THE
COLLECTED POEMS
OF
SARA TEASDALE

BOOKS BY SARA TEASDALE

SONNETS TO DUSE (out of print)

HELEN OF TROY AND OTHER POEMS

RIVERS TO THE SEA

LOVE SONGS

FLAME AND SHADOW

DARK OF THE MOON

STARS TO-NIGHT

STRANGE VICTORY

ANTHOLOGIES

THE ANSWERING VOICE: LOVE LYRICS BY WOMEN

RAINBOW GOLD: POEMS OLD AND NEW, SELECTED FOR BOYS AND GIRLS

Photograph by Nickolas Muray

SARA TEASDALE

The

Collected Poems

of

Sara Teasdale

*

New York

The Macmillan Company

1937

PRINTED IN THE UNITED STATES OF AMERICA
BY THE STRATFORD PRESS, INC., NEW YORK

Contents

. . v . .

Sonnets and Lyrics

Rivers to the Sea (1915)

IV

V

Love Songs (1917)

I

II *Interlude: Songs Out of Sorrow*

III

IV

Flame and Shadow (1920)

I

II *Memories*

III

IV *In a Hospital*

. . x . .

VIII

IX *By the Sea*

X

XI

XII *Songs for Myself*

Dark of the Moon (1926)

I *There Will Be Stars*

II *Pictures of Autumn*

III *Sand Drift*

IV *Portraits*

Stars To-night (1930)
Verses for Boys and Girls

Strange Victory (1933)
I

II

. . xv . .

Sonnets to Duse

AND OTHER POEMS

(1907)

TO ELEONORA DUSE

Oh beauty that is filled so full of tears,
Where every passing anguish left its trace,
I pray you grant to me this depth of grace:
That I may see before it disappears,
Blown through the gateway of our hopes and fears
To death's insatiable last embrace,
The glory and the sadness of your face,
Its longing unappeased through all the years.
No bitterness beneath your sorrow clings;
Within the wild dark falling of your hair
There lies a strength that ever soars and sings;
Your mouth's mute weariness is not despair.
Perhaps among us craven earth-born things
God loves its silence better than a prayer.

TO A PICTURE OF ELEONORA DUSE
IN "THE DEAD CITY"

Your face is set against a fervent sky,
Before the thirsty hills that sevenfold
Return the sun's hot glory, gold on gold,
Where Agamemnon and Cassandra lie.
Your eyes are blind whose light shall never die,
And all the tears the closèd eyelids hold,
And all the longing that the eyes have told,
Is gathered in the lips that make no cry.
Yea, like a flower within a desert place,
Whose petals fold and fade for lack of rain,
Are these, your eyes, where joy of sight was slain,
And in the silence of your lifted face,
The cloud is rent that hides a sleeping race,
And vanished Grecian beauty lives again.

· · 3 · ·

TO A PICTURE OF ELEONORA DUSE
IN "THE DEAD CITY"

Carved in the silence by the hand of Pain,
And made more perfect by the gift of Peace,
Than if Delight had bid your sorrow cease,
And brought the dawn to where the dark has lain,
And set a smile upon your lips again;
Oh strong and noble! Tho' your woes increase,
The gods shall hear no crying for release,
Nor see the tremble that your lips restrain.
Alone as all the chosen are alone,
Yet one with all the beauty of the past;
A sister to the noblest that we know,
The Venus carved in Melos long ago,
Yea, speak to her, and at your lightest tone,
Her lips will part and words will come at last.

TO A PICTURE OF ELEONORA DUSE AS
"FRANCESCA DA RIMINI"

Oh flower-sweet face and bended flower-like head!
Oh violet whose purple cannot pale,
Or forest fragrance ever faint or fail,
Or breath and beauty pass among the dead!
Yea, very truly has the poet said,
No mist of years or might of death avail
To darken beauty—brighter thro' the veil
We see the glimmer of its wings outspread.
Oh face embowered and shadowed by thy hair,
Some lotus blossom on a darkened stream!
If ever I have pictured in a dream
My guardian angel, she is like to this,
Her eyes know joy, yet sorrow lingers there,
And on her lips the shadow of a kiss.

. . 4 . .

THE GIFT

What can I give you, my lord, my lover,
You who have given the world to me,
Showed me the light and the joy that cover
The wild sweet earth and the restless sea?

All that I have are gifts of your giving—
If I gave them again, you would find them old,
And your soul would weary of always living
Before the mirror my life would hold.

What shall I give you, my lord, my lover?
The gift that breaks the heart in me:
I bid you awake at dawn and discover
I have gone my way and left you free.

TO JOY

Lo, I am happy, for my eyes have seen
Joy glowing here before me, face to face;
His wings were arched above me for a space,
I kissed his lips, no bitter came between.
The air is vibrant where his feet have been,
And full of song and color is his place.
His wondrous presence sheds about a grace
That lifts and hallows all that once was mean.
I may not sorrow for I saw the light,
Tho' I shall walk in valley ways for long,
I still shall hear the echo of the song,—
My life is measured by its one great height.
Joy holds more grace than pain can ever give,
And by my glimpse of joy my soul shall live.

· · 5 · ·

ROSES AND RUE

Bring me the roses white and red,
    And take the laurel leaves away;
Yea, wreathe the roses round my head
    That wearies 'neath the crown of bay.

"We searched the wintry forests thro'
    And found no roses anywhere—
But we have brought a little rue
    To twine a circlet for your hair."

I would not pluck the rose in May,
    I wove a laurel crown instead;
And when the crown is cast away,
    They bring me rue—the rose is dead.

FAULTS

They came to tell your faults to me,
They named them over one by one;
I laughed aloud when they were done,
I knew them all so well before,—
Oh, they were blind, too blind to see
Your faults had made me love you more.

Helen of Troy

AND OTHER POEMS
(1911)

Wild flight on flight against the fading dawn
The flames' red wings soar upward duskily.
This is the funeral pyre and Troy is dead
That sparkled so the day I saw it first,
And darkened slowly after. I am she
Who loves all beauty—yet I wither it.
Why have the high gods made me wreak their wrath—
Forever since my maidenhood to sow
Sorrow and blood about me? See, they keep
Their bitter care above me even now.
It was the gods who led me to this lair,
That though the burning winds should make me weak,
They should not snatch the life from out my lips.
Olympus let the other women die;
They shall be quiet when the day is done
And have no care to-morrow. Yet for me
There is no rest. The gods are not so kind
To her made half immortal like themselves.

It is to you I owe the cruel gift,
Leda, my mother, and the Swan, my sire,
To you the beauty and to you the bale;
For never woman born of man and maid
Had wrought such havoc on the earth as I,
Or troubled heaven with a sea of flame
That climbed to touch the silent whirling stars,
Blotting their brightness out before the dawn.
Have I not made the world to weep enough?
Give death to me.
                    Yet life is more than death;
How could I leave the sound of singing winds,
The strong clean scent that breathes from off the sea,

Or shut my eyes forever to the spring?
I will not give the grave my hands to hold,
My shining hair to light oblivion.
Have those who wander through the ways of death,
The still wan fields Elysian, any love
To lift their breasts with longing, any lips
To thirst against the quiver of a kiss?
I shall live on to conquer Greece again,
To make the people love, who hate me now.
My dreams are over, I have ceased to cry
Against the fate that made men love my mouth
And left their spirits all too deaf to hear
The songs that echoed always in my soul.

I have no anger now. The dreams are done;
Yet since the Greeks and Trojans would not see
Aught but my body's fairness, till the end,
In all the islands set in all the seas,
And all the lands that lie beneath the sun,
Till light turn darkness, and till time shall sleep,
Men's lives shall waste with longing after me,
For I shall be the sum of their desire,
The whole of beauty, never seen again.
And they shall stretch their arms and starting, wake,
With "Helen!" on their lips, and in their eyes
The vision of me. Always I shall be
Limned on the darkness like a shaft of light
That glimmers and is gone. They shall behold
Each one his dream that fashions me anew;—
With hair like lakes that glint beneath the stars
Dark as sweet midnight, or with hair aglow
Like burnished gold that still retains the fire.
I shall be haunting till the dusk of time
The heavy eyelids that are filled with dreams.

I wait for one who comes with sword to slay—
The king I wronged who searches for me now;
And yet he shall not slay me. I shall stand
With lifted head and look into his eyes,
Baring my breast to him and to the sun.
He shall not have the power to stain with blood
That whiteness—for the thirsty sword shall fall
And he shall cry and catch me in his arms.
I shall go back to Sparta on his breast.
I shall live on to conquer Greece again!

BEATRICE

Send out the singers—let the room be still;
They have not eased my pain nor brought me sleep,
Close out the sun, for I would have it dark
That I may feel how black the grave will be.
The sun is setting, for the light is red,
And you are outlined in a golden fire,
Like Ursula upon an altar-screen.
Come, leave the light and sit beside my bed,
For I have had enough of saints and prayers.
Strange broken thoughts are beating in my brain,
They come and vanish and again they come.
It is the fever driving out my soul,
And Death stands waiting by the arras there.

Ornella, I will speak, for soon my lips
Shall keep a silence till the end of time.
You have a mouth for loving—listen then:
Keep tryst with Love before Death comes to tryst;
For I, who die, could wish that I had lived
A little closer to the world of men,

Not watching always through the blazoned panes
That show the world in chilly greens and blues
And grudge the sunshine that would enter in.
I was no part of all the troubled crowd
That moved beneath the palace windows here,
And yet sometimes a knight in shining steel
Would pass and catch the gleaming of my hair,
And wave a mailèd hand and smile at me.
I made no sign to him and turned away,
Frightened and yet glad and full of dreams.
Ah, dreams and dreams that asked no answering!
I should have wrought to make my dreams come true.
But all my life was like an autumn day,
Full of gray quiet and a hazy peace.

What was I saying? All is gone again.
It seemed but now I was the little child
Who played within a garden long ago.
Beyond the walls the festal trumpets blared.
Perhaps they carried some Madonna by
With tossing ensigns in a sea of flowers,
A painted Virgin with a painted Child,
Who saw for once the sweetness of the sun
Before they shut her in an altar-niche
Where tapers smoke against the windy gloom.
I gathered roses redder than my gown
And played that I was Saint Elizabeth,
Whose wine had turned to roses in her hands.
And as I played, a child came through the gate,
A boy who looked at me without a word,
As though he saw stretch far behind my head,
Long lines of radiant angels, row on row.
That day we spoke a little, timidly,
And after that I never heard his voice;

Never again in after years his voice
That sang so many songs for love of me.
He was content to stand and watch me pass,
To seek for me at matins every day,
Where I could feel his eyes, although I prayed.
I think if he had stretched his hands to me,
Or moved his lips to say a single word,
I might have loved him. . . .

Ornella, are you there? I cannot see—
Is every one so lonely when he dies?

The room is filled with lights—with waving lights—
Who are the men and women round the bed?
What have I said, Ornella? Have they heard?
There was no evil hidden in my life,
And yet, oh never, never let them know—

Am I not floating in a mist of light?
Oh, lift me up and I shall reach the sun!

MARIANNA ALCOFORANDO

(The Portuguese Nun—1640–1723)

The sparrows wake beneath the convent eaves;
I think I have not slept the whole night through.
But I am old; the agèd scarcely know
The times they wake and sleep, for life burns down;
They breathe the calm of death before they die.
The long night ends, the day comes creeping in,
Showing the sorrows that the darkness hid,
The bended head of Christ, the blood, the thorns,
The wall's gray stains of damp, the pallet bed

Where little Sister Marta dreams of saints,
Waking with arms outstretched imploringly
That seek to stay a vision's vanishing.

I never had a vision, yet for me
Our Lady smiled while all the convent slept
One winter midnight hushed around with snow—
I thought she might be kinder than the rest,
And so I came to kneel before her feet,
Sick with love's sorrow and love's bitterness.
But when I would have made the blessèd sign,
I found the water frozen in the font,
And touched sharp ice within the curving stone.
The saints had hid themselves away from me,
And left the windows black against the night;
And when I sank upon the altar steps
Before the Virgin Mother and her Child,
The last, pale, low-burnt taper flickered out,
But in the darkness, smooth and fathomless,
Still like a star the holy lamp was twinkling
That cast a dusky glow upon her face.
Then through the numbing cold, peace fell on me,
Submission and the gracious gift of tears,
For when I looked, Oh! blessèd miracle,
Her lips had parted and Our Lady smiled!
And then I knew that Love is worth its pain
And that my heart was richer for his sake,
Since lack of love is bitterest of all.

The day is broad awake—the first long beam
Of level sun finds Sister Marta's face,
And trembling there it lights a timid smile
Upon the lips that say so many prayers,
And have no words for hate and none for love.

But when she passes where her prayers have gone,
Will God not smile a little sadly then,
And send her back with gentle words to earth
That she may hold a child against her breast
And feel its small, warm hands upon her hair?

We weep before the blessèd Mother's shrine,
To think upon her sorrows, but her joys
What nun could ever know a tithing of?
The precious hours she watched above His sleep
Were worth the fearful anguish of the end;
Yes, lack of love is bitterest of all.
Yet I have felt what thing it is to know
One thought forever, sleeping or awake;
To say one name whose sweetness grows so wild
That it might work a spell on those who weep;
To feel the weight of love upon my heart
So heavy that the blood can scarcely flow.

Love comes to some unlooked-for, quietly,
As when at twilight, with a soft surprise,
We see the new-born crescent in the blue;
And unto others love is planet-like,
A cold and placid gleam that never wavers;
And there are those who wait the call of love
Expectant of his coming, as we watch
To see the east grow pale before the moon
Lifts up her flower-like head against the night.
But love, for me, was like a cruel sun,
That on some rain-drenched morning, when the leaves
Are bowed beneath their clinging weight of drops,
Tears through the mist, and burns with fervent heat
The tender grasses and the meadow flowers;
Then suddenly the heavy clouds close in

And through the dark the thunder's muttering
Is drowned amid the dashing of the rain.

But I have seen my day grow calm again.
The sun sets slowly on a peaceful world,
And sheds a quiet light across the fields.

GUENEVERE

I was a queen, and I have lost my crown;
A wife, and I have broken all my vows;
A lover, and I ruined him I loved:—
There is no other havoc left to do.
A little month ago I was a queen,
And mothers held their babies up to see
When I came riding out of Camelot.
The women smiled, and all the world smiled too.
And now, what woman's eyes would smile on me?
I am still beautiful, and yet what child
Would think of me as some high, heaven-sent thing,
An angel, clad in gold and miniver?
The world would run from me, and yet I am
No different from the queen they used to love.
If water, flowing silver over stones,
Is forded, and beneath the horses' feet
Grows turbid suddenly, it clears again,
And men will drink it with no thought of harm.
Yet I am branded for a single fault.

I was the flower amid a toiling world,
Where people smiled to see one happy thing,
And they were proud and glad to raise me high;

They only asked that I should be right fair,
A little kind, and gownèd wondrously,
And surely it were little praise to me
If I had pleased them well throughout my life.

I was a queen, the daughter of a king.
The crown was never heavy on my head,
It was my right, and was a part of me.
The women thought me proud, the men were kind,
And bowed down gallantly to kiss my hand,
And watched me as I passed them calmly by,
Along the halls I shall not tread again.
What if, to-night, I should revisit them?
The warders at the gates, the kitchen-maids,
The very beggars would stand off from me,
And I, their queen, would climb the stairs alone,
Pass through the banquet-hall, a hated thing,
And seek my chambers for a hiding-place,
And I should find them but a sepulchre,
The very rushes rotted on the floors,
The fire in ashes on the freezing hearth.

I was a queen, and he who loved me best
Made me a woman for a night and day,
And now I go unqueened forevermore

A queen should never dream on summer nights,
When hovering spells are heavy in the dusk:—
I think no night was ever quite so still,
So smoothly lit with red along the west,
So deeply hushed with quiet through and through.
And strangely clear, and sharply dyed with light,
The trees stood straight against a paling sky,
With Venus burning lamp-like in the west.

I walked alone among a thousand flowers,
That drooped their heads and drowsed beneath the dew,
And all my thoughts were quieted to sleep.
Behind me, on the walk, I heard a step—
I did not know my heart could tell his tread,
I did not know I loved him till that hour.
The garden reeled a little, I was weak,
And in my breast I felt a wild, sick pain.
Quickly he came behind me, caught my arms,
That ached beneath his touch; and then I swayed,
My head fell backward and I saw his face.

All this grows bitter that was once so sweet,
And many mouths must drain the dregs of it,
But none will pity me, nor pity him
Whom Love so lashed, and with such cruel thongs.

ERINNA

They sent you in to say farewell to me,
No, do not shake your head; I see your eyes
That shine with tears. Sappho, you saw the sun
Just now when you came hither; and again,
When you have left me, all the shimmering
Great meadows will laugh lightly, and the sun
Put round about you warm invisible arms
As might a lover, decking you with light.
I go toward darkness though I lie so still.
If I could see the sun, I should look up
And drink the light until my eyes were blind;
I should kneel down and kiss the blades of grass,
And I should call the birds with such a voice,
With such a longing, tremulous and keen,

That they would fly to me and on the breast
Bear evermore to tree-tops and to fields
The kiss I gave them.

                    Sappho, tell me this,
Was I not sometimes fair? My eyes, my mouth,
My hair that loved the wind, were they not worth
The breath of love upon them? Yet he passed,
And he will pass to-night when all the air
Is blue with twilight; but I shall not see.
I shall have gone forever. Hold my hands,
Hold fast, that Death may never come between;
Swear by the gods you will not let me go;
Make songs for Death as you would sing to Love—
But you will not assuage him. He alone
Of all the gods will take no gifts from men.
I am afraid, afraid.
                    Sappho, lean down.
Last night the fever gave a dream to me,
It takes my life and gives me only a dream.
I thought I saw him stand, the man I love,
Here in my quiet chamber, with his eyes
Fixed on me as I entered, while he drew
Silently toward me—he who night by night
Goes by my door without a thought of me—
Neared me and put his hand behind my head,
And leaning toward me, kissed me on the mouth.
That was a little dream for Death to give,
Too short to take the whole of life for, yet
I woke with lips made quiet by a kiss.

The dream is worth the dying. Do not smile
So sadly on me with your shining eyes,
You who can set your sorrow to a song

· ·   19   · ·

And ease your hurt by singing. But to me
My songs are less than sea-sand that the wind
Drives stinging over me and bears away.
I have no care what place the grains may fall,
Nor of my songs, if Time shall blow them back,
As land-wind breaks the lines of dying foam
Along the bright wet beaches, scattering
The flakes once more against the laboring sea,
Into oblivion. What do I care
To please Apollo since Love does not hear?
Your words will live forever, men will say
"She was the perfect lover"—I shall die,
I loved too much to live. Go Sappho, go—
I hate your hands that beat so full of life,
Go, lest my hatred hurt you. I shall die,
But you will live to love and love again.
He might have loved some other spring than this;
I should have kept my life—I let it go.
He would not love me now though Cypris bound
Her girdle round me. I am Death's, not Love's.
Go from me, Sappho, back to find the sun.

I am alone, alone. O Cyprian . . .

SONG

You bound strong sandals on my feet,
　　You gave me bread and wine,
And sent me under sun and stars,
　　For all the world was mine.

Oh, take the sandals off my feet,
　　You know not what you do;
For all my world is in your arms,
　　My sun and stars are you.

WILD ASTERS

In the spring I asked the daisies
　　If his words were true,
And the clever little daisies
　　Always knew.

Now the fields are brown and barren,
　　Bitter autumn blows,
And of all the stupid asters
　　Not one knows.

THE SHRINE

There is no lord within my heart,
　　Left silent as an empty shrine
　　Where rose and myrtle intertwine,
Within a place apart.

No god is there of carven stone
　　To watch with still approving eyes
　　My thoughts like steady incense rise;
I dream and weep alone.

But if I keep my altar fair,
    Some morning I shall lift my head
    From roses deftly garlanded
To find the god is there.

LOVE ME

Brown-thrush singing all day long
    In the leaves above me,
Take my love this April song,
    "Love me, love me, love me!"

When he harkens what you say,
    Bid him, lest he miss me,
Leave his work or leave his play,
    And kiss me, kiss me, kiss me!

THE SONG FOR COLIN

I sang a song at dusking time
    Beneath the evening star,
And Terence left his latest rhyme
    To answer from afar.

Pierrot laid down his lute to weep,
    And sighed, "She sings for me,"
But Colin slept a careless sleep
    Beneath an apple tree.

FOUR WINDS

"Four winds blowing through the sky,
You have seen poor maidens die,

Tell me then what I shall do
That my lover may be true."
Said the wind from out the south,
"Lay no kiss upon his mouth,"
And the wind from out the west,
"Wound the heart within his breast,"
And the wind from out the east,
"Send him empty from the feast,"
And the wind from out the north,
"In the tempest thrust him forth,
When thou art more cruel than he,
Then will Love be kind to thee."

DEW

I dream that he is mine,
    I dream that he is true,
And all his words I keep
    As rose-leaves hold the dew.

O little thirsty rose,
    O little heart beware,
Lest you should hope to hold
    A hundred roses' share.

A MAIDEN

Oh if I were the velvet rose
    Upon the red rose vine,
I'd climb to touch his window
    And make his casement fine.

And if I were the bright-eyed bird
    That twitters on the tree,

All day I'd sing my love for him
　　Till he should harken me.

But since I am a maiden
　　I go with downcast eyes,
And he will never hear the songs
　　That he has turned to sighs.

And since I am a maiden
　　My love will never know
That I could kiss him with a mouth
　　More red than roses blow.

I LOVE YOU

When April bends above me
　　And finds me fast asleep,
Dust need not keep the secret
　　A live heart died to keep.

When April tells the thrushes,
　　The meadow-larks will know,
And pipe the three words lightly
　　To all the winds that blow.

Above his roof the swallows,
　　In notes like far-blown rain,
Will tell the chirping sparrow
　　Beside his window-pane.

O sparrow, little sparrow,
　　When I am fast asleep,
Then tell my love the secret
　　That I have died to keep.

BUT NOT TO ME

The April night is still and sweet
    With flowers on every tree;
Peace comes to them on quiet feet,
    But not to me.

My peace is hidden in his breast
    Where I shall never be,
Loves come to-night to all the rest,
    But not to me.

YOUTH AND THE PILGRIM

Gray pilgrim, you have journeyed far,
    Swear on my sword to me,
Is there a land where Love is not,
    By shore of any sea?

For I am weary of the god,
    And I would flee from him
Though I must take a ship and go
    Beyond the ocean's rim.

"There is a place where Love is not,
    But never a ship leaves land .
Can carry you so quickly there
    As the sharp sword in your hand."

THE WANDERER

I saw the sunset-colored sands,
    The Nile like flowing fire between,
    Where Rameses stares forth serene,
And Ammon's heavy temple stands.

I saw the rocks where long ago,
  Above the sea that cries and breaks,
  Bright Perseus with Medusa's snakes
Set free the maiden white like snow.

And many skies have covered me,
  And many winds have blown me forth,
  And I have loved the green, bright north,
And I have loved the cold, sweet sea.

But what to me are north and south,
  And what the lure of many lands,
  Since you have leaned to catch my hands
And lay a kiss upon my mouth.

"I WOULD LIVE IN YOUR LOVE"

I would live in your love as the sea-grasses live in the sea,
Borne up by each wave as it passes, drawn down by each wave
    that recedes;
I would empty my soul of the dreams that have gathered
    in me,
I would beat with your heart as it beats, I would follow your
    soul as it leads.

MAY

The wind is tossing the lilacs,
  The new leaves laugh in the sun,
And the petals fall on the orchard wall,
  But for me the spring is done.

Beneath the apple blossoms
  I go a wintry way,
For love that smiled in April
  Is false to me in May.

"LESS THAN THE CLOUD TO THE WIND"

Less than the cloud to the wind,
  Less than the foam to the sea,
Less than the rose to the storm
  Am I to thee.

More than the star to the night,
  More than the rain to the tree,
More than heaven to earth
  Art thou to me.

PIERROT

Pierrot stands in the garden
  Beneath a waning moon,
And on his lute he fashions
  A fragile silver tune.

Pierrot plays in the garden,
  He thinks he plays for me,
But I am quite forgotten
  Under the cherry tree.

Pierrot plays in the garden,
  And all the roses know
That Pierrot loves his music,—
  But I love Pierrot.

AT NIGHT

Love said, "Lie still and think of me,"
  Sleep, "Close your eyes till break of day,"
But Dreams came by and smilingly
  Gave both to Love and Sleep their way.

· · 29 · ·

THE KISS

I hoped that he would love me,
    And he has kissed my mouth,
But I am like a stricken bird
    That cannot reach the south.

For though I know he loves me,
    To-night my heart is sad;
His kiss was not so wonderful
    As all the dreams I had.

NOVEMBER

The world is tired, the year is old,
    The faded leaves are glad to die,
The wind goes shivering with cold
    Where the brown reeds are dry.

Our love is dying like the grass,
    And we who kissed grow coldly kind,
Half glad to see our poor love pass
    Like leaves along the wind.

THE WIND

A wind is blowing over my soul,
    I hear it cry the whole night through—
Is there no peace for me on earth
    Except with you?

Alas, the wind has made me wise,
    Over my naked soul it blew,—
There is no peace for me on earth
    Even with you.

A WINTER NIGHT

My window-pane is starred with frost,
  The world is bitter cold to-night,
The moon is cruel, and the wind
  Is like a two-edged sword to smite.

God pity all the homeless ones,
  The beggars pacing to and fro,
God pity all the poor to-night
  Who walk the lamp-lit streets of snow.

My room is like a bit of June,
  Warm and close-curtained fold on fold,
But somewhere, like a homeless child,
  My heart is crying in the cold.

THE METROPOLITAN TOWER

We walked together in the dusk
  To watch the tower grow dimly white,
And saw it lift against the sky
  Its flower of amber light.

You talked of half a hundred things,
  I kept each hurried word you said;
And when at last the hour was full,
  I saw the light turn red.

You did not know the time had come,
  You did not see the sudden flower,
Nor know that in my heart Love's birth
  Was reckoned from that hour.

GRAMERCY PARK

The little park was filled with peace,
  The walks were carpeted with snow,
But every iron gate was locked,
  Lest if we entered, peace would go.

We circled it a dozen times,
  The wind was blowing from the sea,
I only felt your restless eyes
  Whose love was like a cloak for me.

Oh heavy gates that fate has locked
  To bar the joy we can not win.
Peace would go out forever
  If we should enter in.

IN THE METROPOLITAN MUSEUM

Inside the tiny Pantheon
  We stood together silently,
Leaving the restless crowd awhile
  As ships find shelter from the sea.

The ancient centuries came back
  To cover us a moment's space,
And through the dome the light was glad
  Because it shone upon your face.

Ah, not from Rome but farther still,
  Beyond sun-smitten Salamis,
The moment took us, till you leaned
  To find the present with a kiss.

· · 32 · ·

CONEY ISLAND

Why did you bring me here?
The sand is white with snow,
Over the wooden domes
The winter sea-winds blow—
There is no shelter near,
　　Come, let us go.

With foam of icy lace
The sea creeps up the sand,
The wind is like a hand
That strikes us in the face.
Doors that June set a-swing
Are bolted long ago;
We try them uselessly—
Alas, there cannot be
For us a second spring;
　　Come, let us go.

UNION SQUARE

With the man I love who loves me not,
　I walked in the street-lamps' flare;
We watched the world go home that night
　In a flood through Union Square.

I leaned to catch the words he said
　That were light as a snowflake falling;
Ah well that he never leaned to hear
　The words my heart was calling.

And on we walked and on we walked
　Past the fiery lights of the picture shows—

Where the girls with thirsty eyes go by
   On the errand each man knows.

And on we walked and on we walked,
   At the door at last we said good-bye;
I knew by his smile he had not heard
   My heart's unuttered cry.

With the man I love who loves me not
   I walked in the street-lamps' flare—
But oh, the girls who ask for love
   In the lights of Union Square.

CENTRAL PARK AT DUSK

Buildings above the leafless trees
   Loom high as castles in a dream,
While one by one the lamps come out
   To thread the twilight with a gleam.

There is no sign of leaf or bud,
   A hush is over everything—
Silent as women wait for love,
   The world is waiting for the spring.

SONNETS AND LYRICS

As kings, seeing their lives about to pass,
Take off the heavy ermine and the crown,
So had the trees that autumn-time laid down
Their golden garments on the dying grass,
When I, who watched the seasons in the glass
Of my own thoughts, saw all the autumn's brown
Leap into life and wear a sunny gown
Of leafage fresh as happy April has.
Great spring came singing upward from the south;
For in my heart, far carried on the wind,
Your words like wingèd seeds took root and grew,
And all the world caught music from your mouth;
I saw the light as one who had been blind,
And knew my sun and song and spring were you.

FOR THE ANNIVERSARY OF JOHN KEATS' DEATH
(February 23, 1821)

At midnight, when the moonlit cypress trees
Have woven round his grave a magic shade,
Still weeping the unfinished hymn he made,
There moves fresh Maia, like a morning breeze
Blown over jonquil beds when warm rains cease.
And stooping where her poet's head is laid,
Selene weeps, while all the tides are stayed,
And swaying seas are darkened into peace.
But they who wake the meadows and the tides
Have hearts too kind to bid him wake from sleep,
Who murmurs sometimes when his dreams are deep,
Startling the Quiet Land where he abides,
And charming still sad-eyed Persephone
With visions of the sunny earth and sea.

TO AN ÆOLIAN HARP

The winds have grown articulate in thee,
And voiced again the wail of ancient woe
That smote upon the winds of long ago;
The cries of Trojan women as they flee,
The quivering moan of pale Andromache,
Now lifted loud with pain and now brought low.
It is the soul of sorrow that we know,
As in a shell the soul of all the sea.
So sometimes in the compass of a song,
Unknown to him who sings, through lips that live,
The voiceless dead of long-forgotten lands
Proclaim to us their heaviness and wrong
In sweeping sadness of the winds that give
Thy strings no rest from weariless wild hands.

TO ERINNA

Was Time not harsh to you, or was he kind,
O pale Erinna of the perfect lyre,
That he has left no word of singing fire
Whereby you waked the dreaming Lesbian wind,
And kindled night along the darkened shore?
O girl whose lips Erato stooped to kiss,
Do you go sorrowing because of this
In fields where poets sing forevermore?
Or are you glad, and is it best to be
A silent music men have never heard,
A dream in all our hearts that we may say:
"Her voice had all the rapture of the sea,
And all the clear cool quiver of a bird
Deep in a forest at the break of day"?

TO CLEÏS

(The daughter of Sappho)

When the dusk was wet with dew,
  Cleïs, did the muses nine
  Listen in a silent line
While your mother sang to you?

Did they weep or did they smile
  When she crooned to still your cries,
  She, a muse in human guise,
Who forsook her lyre awhile?

Did you feel her wild heart beat?
  Did the warmth of all the sun
  Through your little body run
When she kissed your hands and feet?

Did your fingers, babywise,
  Touch her face and touch her hair,
  Did you think your mother fair,
Could you bear her burning eyes?

Are the songs that soothed your fears
  Vanished like a vanished flame,
  Save the line where shines your name
Starlike down the graying years? . . .

Cleïs speaks no word to me,
  For the land where she has gone
  Lies as still at dusk and dawn
As a windless, tideless sea.

PARIS IN SPRING

The city 's all a-shining
    Beneath a fickle sun,
A gay young wind 's a-blowing,
    The little shower is done.
But the rain-drops still are clinging
    And falling one by one—
Oh, it 's Paris, it 's Paris,
    And spring-time has begun.

I know the Bois is twinkling
    In a sort of hazy sheen,
And down the Champs the gray old arch
    Stands cold and still between.
But the walk is flecked with sunlight
    Where the great acacias lean,
Oh, it 's Paris, it 's Paris,
    And the leaves are growing green.

The sun 's gone in, the sparkle 's dead,
    There falls a dash of rain,
But who would care when such an air
    Comes blowing up the Seine?
And still Ninette sits sewing
    Beside her window-pane,
When it 's Paris, it 's Paris,
    And spring-time 's come again.

MADEIRA FROM THE SEA

Out of the delicate dream of the distance an emerald emerges
Veiled in the violet folds of the air of the sea;
Softly the dream grows awakening—shimmering white of a
    city,

Splashes of crimson, the gay bougainvillea, the palms.
High in the infinite blue of its heaven a quiet cloud lingers,
Lost and forgotten by winds that have fallen asleep,
Fallen asleep to the tune of a Portuguese song in a garden.

CITY VIGNETTES

I

DAWN

The greenish sky glows up in misty reds,
   The purple shadows turn to brick and stone,
The dreams wear thin, men turn upon their beds,
   And hear the milk-cart jangle by alone.

II

DUSK

The city's street, a roaring, blackened stream,
   Walled in by granite, through whose thousand eyes
A thousand yellow lights begin to gleam,
   And over all the pale, untroubled skies.

III

RAIN AT NIGHT

The street-lamps shine in a yellow line
   Down the splashy, gleaming street,
And the rain is heard, now loud, now blurred
   By the tread of homing feet.

The beast to the beast is calling,
   And the mind bends down to wait;
Like the stealthy lord of the jungle,
   The man calls to his mate.

The beast to the beast is calling,
   They rush through the twilight sweet—
But the mind is a wary hunter;
   He will not let them meet.

CHRISTMAS CAROL

The kings they came from out the south,
   All dressed in ermine fine;
They bore Him gold and chrysoprase,
   And gifts of precious wine.

The shepherds came from out the north,
   Their coats were brown and old;
They brought Him little new-born lambs—
   They had not any gold.

The wise men came from out the east,
   And they were wrapped in white;
The star that led them all the way
   Did glorify the night.

The angels came from heaven high,
   And they were clad with wings;
And lo, they brought a joyful song
   The host of heaven sings.

The kings they knocked upon the door,
   The wise men entered in,
The shepherds followed after them
   To hear the song begin.

The angels sang through all the night
   Until the rising sun,
But little Jesus fell asleep
   Before the song was done.

"THE FAËRY FOREST"

The faëry forest glimmered
   Beneath an ivory moon,
The silver grasses shimmered
   Against a faëry tune.

Beneath the silken silence
   The crystal branches slept,
And dreaming through the dew-fall
   The cold, white blossoms wept.

A MINUET OF MOZART'S

Across the dimly lighted room
   The violin drew wefts of sound;
   Airily they wove and wound
And glimmered gold against the gloom.

I watched the music turn to light,
   But at the pausing of the bow,
   The web was broken, and the glow
Was drowned within the wave of night.

· · 43 · ·

TWILIGHT

Dreamily over the roofs,
   The cold spring rain is falling;
Out in the lonely tree
   A bird is calling, calling.

Slowly over the earth,
   The wings of night are falling;
My heart, like the bird in the tree,
   Is calling, calling, calling.

Rivers to the Sea
(1915)

I

SPRING NIGHT

The park is filled with night and fog,
    The veils are drawn about the world,
The drowsy lights along the paths
    Are dim and pearled.

Gold and gleaming the empty streets,
    Gold and gleaming the misty lake,
The mirrored lights like sunken swords,
    Glimmer and shake.

Oh, is it not enough to be
Here with this beauty over me?
My throat should ache with praise, and I
Should kneel in joy beneath the sky.
O, beauty are you not enough?
Why am I crying after love,
With youth, a singing voice and eyes
To take earth's wonder with surprise?
Why have I put off my pride,
Why am I unsatisfied,—
I for whom the pensive night
Binds her cloudy hair with light,—
I, for whom all beauty burns
Like incense in a million urns?
O, beauty, are you not enough?
Why am I crying after love?

THE FLIGHT

Look back with longing eyes and know that I will follow,
Lift me up in your love as a light wind lifts a swallow,
Let our flight be far in sun or blowing rain—
But what if I heard my first love calling me again?

Hold me on your heart as the brave sea holds the foam,
Take me far away to the hills that hide your home;
Peace shall thatch the roof and love shall latch the door—
But what if I heard my first love calling me once more?

NEW LOVE AND OLD

In my heart the old love
    Struggled with the new;
It was ghostly waking
    All night through.

Dear things, kind things,
    That my old love said,
Ranged themselves reproachfully
    Round my bed.

But I could not heed them,
    For I seemed to see
The eyes of my new love
    Fixed on me.

Old love, old love,
    How can I be true?
Shall I be faithless to myself
    Or to you?

THE LOOK

Strephon kissed me in the spring,
    Robin in the fall,
But Colin only looked at me
    And never kissed at all.

Strephon's kiss was lost in jest,
       Robin's lost in play,
But the kiss in Colin's eyes
       Haunts me night and day.

THE KISS

Before you kissed me only winds of heaven
       Had kissed me, and the tenderness of rain—
Now you have come, how can I care for kisses
       Like theirs again?

I sought the sea, she sent her winds to meet me,
       They surged about me singing of the south—
I turned my head away to keep still holy
       Your kiss upon my mouth.

And swift sweet rains of shining April weather
       Found not my lips where living kisses are;
I bowed my head lest they put out my glory
       As rain puts out a star.

I am my love's and he is mine forever,
       Sealed with a seal and safe forevermore—
Think you that I could let a beggar enter
       Where a king stood before?

SWANS

Night is over the park, and a few brave stars
       Look on the lights that link it with chains of gold,
The lake bears up their reflection in broken bars
       That seem too heavy for tremulous water to hold.

We watch the swans that sleep in a shadowy place,
  And now and again one wakes and uplifts its head;
How still you are——your gaze is on my face——
  We watch the swans and never a word is said.

THE OLD MAID

I saw her in a Broadway car,
  The woman I might grow to be;
I felt my lover look at her
  And then turn suddenly to me.

Her hair was dull and drew no light
  And yet its color was as mine;
Her eyes were strangely like my eyes
  Tho' love had never made them shine.

Her body was a thing grown thin,
  Hungry for love that never came;
Her soul was frozen in the dark
  Unwarmed forever by love's flame.

I felt my lover look at her
  And then turn suddenly to me,——
His eyes were magic to defy
  The woman I shall never be.

AT NIGHT

We are apart; the city grows quiet between us,
  She hushes herself, for midnight makes heavy her eyes,
The tangle of traffic is ended, the cars are empty,
  Five streets divide us, and on them the moonlight lies.

· · 52 · ·

Oh are you asleep, or lying awake, my lover?
Open your dreams to my love and your heart to my words,
I send you my thoughts—the air between us is laden,
My thoughts fly in at your window, a flock of wild birds.

THE YEARS

To-night I close my eyes and see
A strange procession passing me—
The years before I saw your face
Go by me with a wistful grace;
They pass, the sensitive, shy years,
As one who strives to dance, half blind with tears.

The years went by and never knew
That each one brought me nearer you;
Their path was narrow and apart
And yet it led me to your heart—
Oh, sensitive, shy years, oh, lonely years,
That strove to sing with voices drowned in tears.

PEACE

Peace flows into me
As the tide to the pool by the shore;
It is mine forevermore,
It ebbs not back like the sea.

I am the pool of blue
That worships the vivid sky;
My hopes were heaven-high,
They are all fulfilled in you.

I am the pool of gold
   When sunset burns and dies,—
   You are my deepening skies,
Give me your stars to hold.

APRIL

The roofs are shining from the rain,
   The sparrows twitter as they fly,
And with a windy April grace
   The little clouds go by.

Yet the back-yards are bare and brown
   With only one unchanging tree—
I could not be so sure of Spring
   Save that it sings in me.

COME

Come, when the pale moon like a petal
   Floats in the pearly dusk of spring,
Come with arms outstretched to take me,
   Come with lips pursed up to cling.

Come, for life is a frail moth flying
   Caught in the web of the years that pass,
And soon we two, so warm and eager,
   Will be as the gray stones in the grass.

MOODS

I am the still rain falling,
   Too tired for singing mirth—
Oh, be the green fields calling,
   Oh, be for me the earth!

· · 54 · ·

I am the brown bird pining
 To leave the nest and fly—
Oh, be the fresh cloud shining,
 Oh, be for me the sky!

APRIL SONG

Willow in your April gown
 Delicate and gleaming,
Do you mind in years gone by
 All my dreaming?

Spring was like a call to me
 That I could not answer,
I was chained to loneliness,
 I, the dancer.

Willow, twinkling in the sun,
 Still your leaves and hear me,
I can answer spring at last,
 Love is near me!

BROADWAY

This is the quiet hour; the theaters
 Have gathered in their crowds, and steadily
 The million lights blaze on for few to see,
Robbing the sky of stars that should be hers.
A woman waits with bag and shabby furs,
 A somber man drifts by, and only we
 Pass up the street unwearied, warm and free,
For over us the olden magic stirs.

Beneath the liquid splendor of the lights
  We live a little ere the charm is spent;
This night is ours, of all the golden nights,
    The pavement an enchanted palace floor,
  And Youth the player on the viol, who sent
    A strain of music through an open door.

A WINTER BLUEJAY

Crisply the bright snow whispered,
Crunching beneath our feet;
Behind us as we walked along the parkway,
Our shadows danced,
Fantastic shapes in vivid blue.
Across the lake the skaters
Flew to and fro,
With sharp turns weaving
A frail invisible net.
In ecstasy the earth
Drank the silver sunlight;
In ecstasy the skaters
Drank the wine of speed;
In ecstasy we laughed
Drinking the wine of love.
Had not the music of our joy
Sounded its highest note?
But no,
For suddenly, with lifted eyes you said,
"Oh look!"
There, on the black bough of a snow flecked maple,
Fearless and gay as our love,
A bluejay cocked his crest!
Oh who can tell the range of joy
Or set the bounds of beauty?

IN A RESTAURANT

The darkened street was muffled with the snow,
  The falling flakes had made your shoulders white,
  And when we found a shelter from the night
Its glamor fell upon us like a blow.
The clash of dishes and the viol and bow
  Mingled beneath the fever of the light.
  The heat was full of savors, and the bright
Laughter of women lured the wine to flow.
A little child ate nothing while she sat
  Watching a woman at a table there
Lean to a kiss beneath a drooping hat.
  The hour went by, we rose and turned to go,
The somber street received us from the glare,
  And once more on your shoulders fell the snow.

JOY

I am wild, I will sing to the trees,
  I will sing to the stars in the sky,
I love, I am loved, he is mine,
  Now at last I can die!

I am sandaled with wind and with flame,
  I have heart-fire and singing to give,
I can tread on the grass or the stars,
  Now at last I can live!

IN A RAILROAD STATION

We stood in the shrill electric light,
  Dumb and sick in the whirling din—
We who had all of love to say
  And a single second to say it in.

· · 57 · ·

"Good-by!" "Good-by!"—you turned to go,
    I felt the train's slow heavy start,—
You thought to see me cry, but oh,
    My tears were hidden in my heart.

IN THE TRAIN

Fields beneath a quilt of snow
    From which the rocks and stubble peep,
And in the west a shy white star
    That shivers as it wakes from sleep.

The restless rumble of the train,
    The drowsy people in the car,
Steel blue twilight in the world,
    And in my heart a timid star.

TO ONE AWAY

I heard a cry in the night,
    A thousand miles it came,
Sharp as a flash of light,
    My name, my name!

It was your voice I heard,
    You waked and loved me so—
I send you back this word,
    I know, I know!

SONG

Love me with your whole heart
    Or give no love to me,
Half-love is a poor thing,
    Neither bond nor free.

You must love me gladly
    Soul and body too,
Or else find a new love,
    And good-by to you.

"DEEP IN THE NIGHT"

Deep in the night the cry of a swallow,
    Under the stars he flew,
Keen as pain was his call to follow
    Over the world to you.

Love in my heart is a cry forever
    Lost as the swallow's flight,
Seeking for you and never, never
    Stilled by the stars at night.

THE INDIA WHARF

Here in the velvet stillness
The wide sown fields fall to the faint horizon,
Sleeping in starlight. . . .

A year ago we walked in the jangling city
Together . . . forgetful.
One by one we crossed the avenues,
Rivers of light, roaring in tumult,
And came to the narrow, knotted streets.
Through the tense crowd
We went aloof, ecstatic, walking in wonder,
Unconscious of our motion.

Forever the foreign people with dark, deep-seeing eyes
Passed us and passed.
Lights and foreign words and foreign faces,
I forgot them all;
I only felt alive, defiant of all death and sorrow,
Sure and elated.

That was the gift you gave me. . . .

The streets grew still more tangled,
And led at last to water black and glossy,
Flecked here and there with lights, faint and far off.
There on a shabby building was a sign
"The India Wharf" . . . and we turned back.

I always felt we could have taken ship
And crossed the bright green seas
To dreaming cities set on sacred streams
And palaces
Of ivory and scarlet.

I SHALL NOT CARE

When I am dead and over me bright April
    Shakes out her rain-drenched hair,
Tho' you should lean above me broken-hearted,
    I shall not care.

I shall have peace, as leafy trees are peaceful
    When rain bends down the bough,
And I shall be more silent and cold-hearted
    Than you are now.

DESERT POOLS

I love too much; I am a river
  Surging with spring that seeks the sea,
I am too generous a giver,
  Love will not stoop to drink of me.

His feet will turn to desert places
  Shadowless, reft of rain and dew,
Where stars stare down with sharpened faces
  From heavens pitilessly blue.

And there at midnight sick with faring,
  He will stoop down in his desire
To slake the thirst grown past all bearing
  In stagnant water keen as fire.

LONGING

I am not sorry for my soul
  That it must go unsatisfied,
For it can live a thousand times,
  Eternity is deep and wide.

I am not sorry for my soul,
  But oh, my body that must go
Back to a little drift of dust
  Without the joy it longed to know.

PITY

They never saw my lover's face,
  They only know our love was brief,
Wearing awhile a windy grace
  And passing like an autumn leaf.

They wonder why I do not weep,
  They think it strange that I can sing,
They say, "Her love was scarcely deep
  Since it has left so slight a sting."

They never saw my love, nor knew
  That in my heart's most secret place
I pity them as angels do
  Men who have never seen God's face.

AFTER PARTING

Oh I have sown my love so wide
  That he will find it everywhere;
It will awake him in the night,
  It will enfold him in the air.

I set my shadow in his sight
  And I have winged it with desire,
That it may be a cloud by day
  And in the night a shaft of fire.

ENOUGH

It is enough for me by day
  To walk the same bright earth with him;
Enough that over us by night
  The same great roof of stars is dim.

I have no care to bind the wind
  Or set a fetter on the sea—
It is enough to feel his love
  Blow by like music over me.

ALCHEMY

I lift my heart as spring lifts up
   A yellow daisy to the rain;
My heart will be a lovely cup
   Altho' it holds but pain.

For I shall learn from flower and leaf
   That color every drop they hold,
To change the lifeless wine of grief
   To living gold.

FEBRUARY

They spoke of him I love
   With cruel words and gay;
My lips kept silent guard
   On all I could not say.

I heard, and down the street
   The lonely trees in the square
Stood in the winter wind
   Patient and bare.

I heard . . . oh voiceless trees
   Under the wind, I knew
The eager terrible spring
   Hidden in you.

DUSK IN JUNE

Evening, and all the birds
   In a chorus of shimmering sound
Are easing their hearts of joy
   For miles around.

The air is blue and sweet,
    The few first stars are white,—
Oh let me like the birds
    Sing before night.

SUMMER NIGHT, RIVERSIDE

In the wild soft summer darkness
How many and many a night we two together
Sat in the park and watched the Hudson
Wearing her lights like golden spangles
Glinting on black satin.
The rail along the curving pathway
Was low in a happy place to let us cross,
And down the hill a tree that dripped with bloom
Sheltered us,
While your kisses and the flowers,
Falling, falling,
Tangled my hair. . . .

The frail white stars moved slowly over the sky.

And now, far off
In the fragrant darkness
The tree is tremulous again with bloom
For June comes back.

To-night what girl
Dreamily before her mirror shakes from her hair
This year's blossoms, clinging in its coils?

IN A SUBWAY STATION

After a year I came again to the place;
The tireless lights and the reverberation,

The angry thunder of trains that burrow the ground,
The hunted, hurrying people were still the same—
But oh, another man beside me and not you!
Another voice and other eyes in mine!
And suddenly I turned and saw again
The gleaming curve of tracks, the bridge above—
They were burned deep into my heart before,
The night I watched them to avoid your eyes,
When you were saying, "Oh, look up at me!"
When you were saying, "Will you never love me?"
And when I answered with a lie. Oh then
You dropped your eyes. I felt your utter pain.
I would have died to say the truth to you.

*   *   *   *   *   *

After a year I came again to the place—
The hunted hurrying people were still the same. . . .

AFTER LOVE

There is no magic any more,
    We meet as other people do,
You work no miracle for me
    Nor I for you.

You were the wind and I the sea—
    There is no splendor any more,
I have grown listless as the pool
    Beside the shore.

But tho' the pool is safe from storm
    And from the tide has found surcease,
It grows more bitter than the sea,
    For all its peace.

DOORYARD ROSES

I have come the selfsame path
   To the selfsame door,
Years have left the roses there
   Burning as before.

While I watch them in the wind
   Quick the hot tears start—
Strange so frail a flame outlasts
   Fire in the heart.

A PRAYER

Until I lose my soul and lie
   Blind to the beauty of the earth,
Deaf though a shouting wind goes by,
   Dumb in a storm of mirth;

Until my heart is quenched at length
   And I have left the land of men,
Oh, let me love with all my strength
   Careless if I am loved again.

INDIAN SUMMER

Lyric night of the lingering Indian summer,
Shadowy fields that are scentless but full of singing,
Never a bird, but the passionless chant of insects,
    Ceaseless, insistent.

The grasshopper's horn, and far off, high in the maples
The wheel of a locust leisurely grinding the silence,
Under a moon waning and worn and broken,
    Tired with summer.

Let me remember you, voices of little insects,
Weeds in the moonlight, fields that are tangled with asters,
Let me remember you, soon will the winter be on us,
    Snow-hushed and heartless.

Over my soul murmur your mute benediction
While I gaze, oh fields that rest after harvest,
As those who part look long in the eyes they lean to,
    Lest they forget them.

THE SEA WIND

    I am a pool in a peaceful place,
    I greet the great sky face to face,
    I know the stars and the stately moon
    And the wind that runs with rippling shoon—
    But why does it always bring to me
    The far-off, beautiful sound of the sea?

    The marsh-grass weaves me a wall of green,
    But the wind comes whispering in between,

In the dead of night when the sky is deep
The wind comes waking me out of sleep—
Why does it always bring to me
The far-off, terrible call of the sea?

THE CLOUD

I am a cloud in the heaven's height,
The stars are lit for my delight,
Tireless and changeful, swift and free,
I cast my shadow on hill and sea—
But why do the pines on the mountain's crest
Call to me always, "Rest, rest"?

I throw my mantle over the moon
And I blind the sun on his throne at noon,
Nothing can tame me, nothing can bind,
I am a child of the heartless wind—
But oh, the pines on the mountain's crest
Whispering always, "Rest, rest."

THE POORHOUSE

Hope went by and Peace went by
    And would not enter in;
Youth went by and Health went by
    And Love that is their kin.

Those within the house shed tears
    On their bitter bread;
Some were old and some were mad,
    And some were sick a-bed.

Gray Death saw the wretched house
　　And even he passed by—
"They have never lived," he said,
　　"They can wait to die."

DOCTORS

Every night I lie awake
　　And every day I lie abed
And hear the doctors, Pain and Death,
　　Conferring at my head.

They speak in scientific tones,
　　Professional and low—
One argues for a speedy cure,
　　The other, sure and slow.

To one so humble as myself
　　It should be matter for some pride
To have such noted fellows here,
　　Conferring at my side.

THE INN OF EARTH

I came to the crowded Inn of Earth,
　　And called for a cup of wine,
But the Host went by with averted eye
　　From a thirst as keen as mine.

Then I sat down with weariness
　　And asked a bit of bread,
But the Host went by with averted eye
　　And never a word he said.

While always from the outer night
   The waiting souls came in
With stifled cries of sharp surprise
   At all the light and din.

"Then give me a bed to sleep," I said,
   "For midnight comes apace"—
But the Host went by with averted eye
   And I never saw his face.

"Since there is neither food nor rest,
   I go where I fared before"—
But the Host went by with averted eye
   And barred the outer door.

THE MOTHER OF A POET

She is too kind, I think, for mortal things,
Too gentle for the gusty ways of earth;
God gave to her a shy and silver mirth,
And made her soul as clear
And softly singing as an orchard spring's
In sheltered hollows all the sunny year—
A spring that thru the leaning grass looks up
And holds all heaven in its clarid cup,
Mirror to holy meadows high and blue
With stars like drops of dew.

I love to think that never tears at night
Have made her eyes less bright;
That all her girlhood thru
Never a cry of love made over-tense
Her voice's innocence;

That in her hands have lain,
Flowers beaten by the rain,
And little birds before they learned to sing
Drowned in the sudden ecstasy of spring.

I love to think that with a wistful wonder
She held her baby warm against her breast;
That never any fear awoke whereunder
She shuddered at her gift, or trembled lest
Thru the great doors of birth
Here to a windy earth
She lured from heaven a half-unwilling guest.

She caught and kept his first vague flickering smile,
The faint upleaping of his spirit's fire;
And for a long sweet while
In her was all he asked of earth or heaven—
But in the end how far,
Past every shaken star,
Should leap at last that arrow-like desire,
His full-grown manhood's keen
Ardor toward the unseen
Dark mystery beyond the Pleiads seven.

And in her heart she heard
His first dim-spoken word—
She only of them all could understand,
Flushing to feel at last
The silence over-past,
Thrilling as tho' her hand had touched God's hand
But in the end how many words
Winged on a flight she could not follow,
Farther than skyward lark or swallow,
His lips should free to lands she never knew;
Braver than white sea-faring birds

With a fearless melody,
Flying over a shining sea,
A star-white song between the blue and blue.

Oh I have seen a lake as clear and fair
As it were molten air,
Lifting a lily upward to the sun.
How should the water know the glowing heart
That ever to the heaven lifts its fire,
A golden and unchangeable desire?
The water only knows
The faint and rosy glows
Of under-petals, opening apart.
Yet in the soul of earth,
Deep in the primal ground,
Its searching roots are wound,
And centuries have struggled toward its birth.
So, in the man who sings,
All of the voiceless horde
From the cold dawn of things
Have their reward;
All in whose pulses ran
Blood that is his at last,
From the first stooping man
Far in the winnowed past.
Out of the tumult of their love and mating
Each one created, seeing life was good—
Dumb, till at last the song that they were waiting
Breaks like brave April thru a wintry wood.

But what of her whose heart is troubled by it,
The mother who would soothe and set him free,
Fearing the song's storm-shaken ecstasy—
Oh, as the moon that has no power to quiet
The strong wind-driven sea.

IN MEMORIAM F. O. S.

You go a long and lovely journey,
　For all the stars, like burning dew,
Are luminous and luring footprints
　Of souls adventurous as you.

Oh, if you lived on earth elated,
　How is it now that you can run
Free of the weight of flesh and faring
　Far past the birthplace of the sun?

TWILIGHT

The stately tragedy of dusk
　Drew to its perfect close,
The virginal white evening star
　Sank, and the red moon rose.

SWALLOW FLIGHT

I love my hour of wind and light,
　I love men's faces and their eyes,
I love my spirit's veering flight
　Like swallows under evening skies.

THOUGHTS

When I can make my thoughts come forth
　To walk like ladies up and down,
Each one puts on before the glass
　Her most becoming hat and gown.

But oh, the shy and eager thoughts
 That hide and will not get them dressed,
Why is it that they always seem
 So much more lovely than the rest?

THE FOUNTAIN

Oh in the deep blue night
 The fountain sang alone;
It sang to the drowsy heart
 Of the satyr carved in stone.

The fountain sang and sang
 But the satyr never stirred—
Only the great white moon
 In the empty heaven heard.

The fountain sang and sang
 And on the marble rim
The milk-white peacocks slept,
 Their dreams were strange and dim.

Bright dew was on the grass,
 And on the ilex dew,
The dreamy milk-white birds
 Were all a-glisten too.

The fountain sang and sang
 The things one cannot tell,
The dreaming peacocks stirred
 And the gleaming dew-drops fell.

THE ROSE

Beneath my chamber window
Pierrot was singing, singing;
   I heard his lute the whole night thru
     Until the east was red.
Alas, alas, Pierrot,
I had no rose for flinging
   Save one that drank my tears for dew
     Before its leaves were dead.

I found it in the darkness,
I kissed it once and threw it,
   The petals scattered over him,
     His song was turned to joy;
And he will never know—
Alas, the one who knew it!—
   The rose was plucked when dusk was dim
     Beside a laughing boy.

DREAMS

I gave my life to another lover,
   I gave my love, and all, and all—
But over a dream the past will hover,
   Out of a dream the past will call.

I tear myself from sleep with a shiver
   But on my breast a kiss is hot,
And by my bed the ghostly giver
   Is waiting tho' I see him not.

"I AM NOT YOURS"

I am not yours, not lost in you,
   Not lost, although I long to be
Lost as a candle lit at noon,
   Lost as a snowflake in the sea.

You love me, and I find you still
   A spirit beautiful and bright,
Yet I am I, who long to be
   Lost as a light is lost in light.

Oh plunge me deep in love—put out
   My senses, leave me deaf and blind,
Swept by the tempest of your love,
   A taper in a rushing wind.

PIERROT'S SONG

(For a picture by Dugald Walker)

Lady, light in the east hangs low,
   Draw your veils of dream apart,
Under the casement stands Pierrot
   Making a song to ease his heart.
(Yet do not break the song too soon—
   I love to sing in the paling moon.)

The petals are falling, heavy with dew,
   The stars have fainted out of the sky,
Come to me, come, or else I too,
   Faint with the weight of love will die.
(She comes—alas, I hoped to make
   Another stanza for her sake!)

· · 78 · ·

NIGHT IN ARIZONA

The moon is a charring ember
    Dying into the dark;
Off in the crouching mountains
    Coyotes bark.

The stars are heavy in heaven,
    Too great for the sky to hold—
What if they fell and shattered
    The earth with gold?

No lights are over the mesa,
    The wind is hard and wild,
I stand at the darkened window
    And cry like a child.

WHILE I MAY

Wind and hail and veering rain,
    Driven mist that veils the day,
Soul's distress and body's pain,
    I would bear you while I may.

I would love you if I might,
    For so soon my life will be
Buried in a lasting night,
    Even pain denied to me.

DEBT

What do I owe to you
    Who loved me deep and long?
You never gave my spirit wings
    Or gave my heart a song.

But oh, to him I loved
Who loved me not at all,
I owe the open gate
That led thru heaven's wall.

FROM THE NORTH

The northern woods are delicately sweet,
The lake is folded softly by the shore,
But I am restless for the subway's roar,
The thunder and the hurrying of feet.
I try to sleep, but still my eyelids beat
Against the image of the tower that bore
Me high aloft, as if thru heaven's door
I watched the world from God's unshaken seat.
I would go back and breathe with quickened sense
The tunnel's strong hot breath of powdered steel;
But at the ferries I should leave the tense
Dark air behind, and I should mount and be
One among many who are thrilled to feel
The first keen sea-breath from the open sea.

THE LIGHTS OF NEW YORK

The lightning spun your garment for the night
Of silver filaments with fire shot thru,
A broidery of lamps that lit for you
The steadfast splendor of enduring light.
The moon drifts dimly in the heaven's height,
Watching with wonder how the earth she knew
That lay so long wrapped deep in dark and dew,
Should wear upon her breast a star so white.

· · 80 · ·

The festivals of Babylon were dark
    With flaring flambeaux that the wind blew down;
The Saturnalia were a wild boy's lark
    With rain-quenched torches dripping thru the town—
But you have found a god and filched from him
A fire that neither wind nor rain can dim.

SEA LONGING

A thousand miles beyond this sun-steeped wall
    Somewhere the waves creep cool along the sand,
    The ebbing tide forsakes the listless land
With the old murmur, long and musical;
The windy waves mount up and curve and fall,
    And round the rocks the foam blows up like snow,—
    Tho' I am inland far, I hear and know,
For I was born the sea's eternal thrall.
I would that I were there and over me
    The cold insistence of the tide would roll,
    Quenching this burning thing men call the soul,—
Then with the ebbing I should drift and be
    Less than the smallest shell along the shoal,
Less than the sea-gulls calling to the sea.

THE RIVER

I came from the sunny valleys
    And sought for the open sea,
For I thought in its gray expanses
    My peace would come to me.

I came at last to the ocean
    And found it wild and black,
And I cried to the windless valleys,
    "Be kind and take me back!"

· · 81 · ·

But the thirsty tide ran inland,
　　And the salt waves drank of me,
And I who was fresh as the rainfall
　　Am bitter as the sea.

LEAVES

One by one, like leaves from a tree,
All my faiths have forsaken me;
But the stars above my head
Burn in white and delicate red,
And beneath my feet the earth
Brings the sturdy grass to birth.
I who was content to be
But a silken-singing tree,
But a rustle of delight
In the wistful heart of night—
I have lost the leaves that knew
Touch of rain and weight of dew.
Blinded by a leafy crown
I looked neither up nor down—
But the little leaves that die
Have left me room to see the sky;
Now for the first time I know
Stars above and earth below.

THE ANSWER

When I go back to earth
And all my joyous body
Puts off the red and white
That once had been so proud,

If men should pass above
With false and feeble pity,
My dust will find a voice
To answer them aloud:

"Be still, I am content,
Take back your poor compassion,
Joy was a flame in me
Too steady to destroy;
Lithe as a bending reed
Loving the storm that sways her—
I found more joy in sorrow
Than you could find in joy."

OVER THE ROOFS

I

Oh chimes set high on the sunny tower
  Ring on, ring on unendingly,
Make all the hours a single hour,
For when the dusk begins to flower,
  The man I love will come to me! . . .

But no, go slowly as you will,
  I should not bid you hasten so,
For while I wait for love to come,
Some other girl is standing dumb,
  Fearing her love will go.

II

Oh white steam over the roofs, blow high!
  Oh chimes in the tower ring clear and free!
Oh sun awake in the covered sky,
  For the man I love, loves me! . . .

Oh drifting steam disperse and die,
  Oh tower stand shrouded toward the south,—
Fate heard afar my happy cry,
  And laid her finger on my mouth.

III

The dusk was blue with blowing mist,
  The lights were spangles in a veil,
And from the clamor far below
  Floated faint music like a wail.

It voiced what I shall never speak,
  My heart was breaking all night long,
But when the dawn was hard and gray,
  My tears distilled into a song.

IV

I said, "I have shut my heart
  As one shuts an open door,
That Love may starve therein
  And trouble me no more."

But over the roofs there came
  The wet new wind of May,
And a tune blew up from the curb
  Where the street-pianos play.

My room was white with the sun
  And Love cried out in me,
"I am strong, I will break your heart
  Unless you set me free."

A CRY

Oh, there are eyes that he can see,
  And hands to make his hands rejoice,
But to my lover I must be
    Only a voice.

Oh, there are breasts to bear his head,
  And lips whereon his lips can lie,
But I must be till I am dead
    Only a cry.

CHANCE

How many times we must have met
　　Here on the street as strangers do,
Children of chance we were, who passed
　　The door of heaven and never knew.

IMMORTAL

So soon my body will have gone
　　Beyond the sound and sight of men,
And tho' it wakes and suffers now,
　　Its sleep will be unbroken then;
But oh, my frail immortal soul
　　That will not sleep forevermore,
A leaf borne onward by the blast,
　　A wave that never finds the shore.

AFTER DEATH

Now while my lips are living
　　Their words must stay unsaid,
And will my soul remember
　　To speak when I am dead?

Yet if my soul remembered
　　You would not heed it, dear,
For now you must not listen,
　　And then you could not hear.

GIFTS

I gave my first love laughter,
   I gave my second tears,
I gave my third love silence
   Through all the years.

My first love gave me singing,
   My second eyes to see,
But oh, it was my third love
   Who gave my soul to me.

FROM THE SEA

All beauty calls you to me, and you seem,
Past twice a thousand miles of shifting sea,
To reach me. You are as the wind I breathe
Here on the ship's sun-smitten topmost deck,
With only light between the heavens and me.
I feel your spirit and I close my eyes,
Knowing the bright hair blowing in the sun,
The eager whisper and the searching eyes.

*   *   *   *   *   *

Listen, I love you. Do not turn your face
Nor touch me. Only stand and watch awhile
The blue unbroken circle of the sea.
Look far away and let me ease my heart
Of words that beat in it with broken wing.
Look far away, and if I say too much,
Forget that I am speaking. Only watch,
How like a gull that sparkling sinks to rest,
The foam-crest drifts along a happy wave
Toward the bright verge, the boundary of the world.

*   *   *   *   *   *

I am so weak a thing, praise me for this,
That in some strange way I was strong enough
To keep my love unuttered and to stand
Altho' I longed to kneel to you that night
You looked at me with ever-calling eyes.
Was I not calm? And if you guessed my love
You thought it something delicate and free,
Soft as the sound of fir-trees in the wind,
Fleeting as phosphorescent stars in foam.
Yet in my heart there was a beating storm
Bending my thoughts before it, and I strove

To say too little lest I say too much,
And from my eyes to drive love's happy shame.
Yet when I heard your name the first far time
It seemed like other names to me, and I
Was all unconscious, as a dreaming river
That nears at last its long predestined sea;
And when you spoke to me, I did not know
That to my life's high altar came its priest.
But now I know between my God and me
You stand forever, nearer God than I,
And in your hands with faith and utter joy
I would that I could lay my woman's soul.

*   *   *   *   *   *

Oh, my love
To whom I cannot come with any gift
Of body or of soul, I pass and go.
But sometimes when you hear blown back to you
My wistful, far-off singing touched with tears,
Know that I sang for you alone to hear,
And that I wondered if the wind would bring
To him who tuned my heart its distant song.
So might a woman who in loneliness
Had borne a child, dreaming of days to come,
Wonder if it would please its father's eyes.
But long before I ever heard your name,
Always the undertone's unchanging note
In all my singing had prefigured you,
Foretold you as a spark foretells a flame.
Yet I was free as an untethered cloud
In the great space between the sky and sea,
And might have blown before the wind of joy
Like a bright banner woven by the sun.
I did not know the longing in the night—
You who have waked me cannot give me sleep.

All things in all the world can rest, but I,
Even the smooth brief respite of a wave
When it gives up its broken crown of foam,
Even that little rest I may not have.
And yet all quiet loves of friends, all joy
In all the piercing beauty of the world
I would give up—go blind forevermore,
Rather than have God blot from out my soul
Remembrance of your voice that said my name.

*   *   *   *   *   *

For us no starlight stilled the April fields,
No birds awoke in darkling trees for us,
Yet where we walked the city's street that night
Felt in our feet the singing fire of spring,
And in our path we left a trail of light
Soft as the phosphorescence of the sea
When night submerges in the vessel's wake
A heaven of unborn evanescent stars.

VIGNETTES OVERSEAS

I

OFF GIBRALTAR

Beyond the sleepy hills of Spain,
    The sun goes down in yellow mist,
The sky is fresh with dewy stars
    Above a sea of amethyst.

Yet in the city of my love
    High noon burns all the heavens bare—
For him the happiness of light,
    For me a delicate despair.

II

Oh give me neither love nor tears,
   Nor dreams that sear the night with fire,
Go lightly on your pilgrimage
   Unburdened by desire.

Forget me for a month, a year,
   But, oh, belovèd, think of me
When unexpected beauty burns
   Like sudden sunlight on the sea.

III

NAPLES

Nisida and Prosida are laughing in the light,
Capri is a dewy flower lifting into sight,
Posilipo kneels and looks in the burnished sea,
Naples crowds her million roofs close as close can be;
Round about the mountain's crest a flag of smoke is hung—
Oh when God made Italy he was gay and young!

IV

CAPRI

When beauty grows too great to bear
   How shall I ease me of its ache,
For beauty more than bitterness
   Makes the heart break.

Now while I watch the dreaming sea
   With isles like flowers against her breast,
Only one voice in all the world
   Could give me rest.

V

I asked the heaven of stars
    What I should give my love—
It answered me with silence,
    Silence above.

I asked the darkened sea
    Down where the fishers go—
It answered me with silence,
    Silence below.

Oh, I could give him weeping,
    Or I could give him song—
But how can I give silence
    My whole life long?

VI

RUINS OF PAESTUM

On lowlands where the temples lie
    The marsh-grass mingles with the flowers,
Only the little songs of birds
    Link the unbroken hours.

So in the end, above my heart
    Once like the city wild and gay,
The slow white stars will pass by night,
    The swift brown birds by day.

VII

ROME

Oh for the rising moon
    Over the roofs of Rome,
And swallows in the dusk
    Circling a darkened dome!

Oh for the measured dawns
That pass with folded wings—
How can I let them go
With unremembered things?

VIII

FLORENCE

The bells ring over the Arno,
Midnight, the long, long chime;
Here in the quivering darkness
I am afraid of time.

Oh, gray bells cease your tolling,
Time takes too much from me,
And yet to rock and river
He gives eternity.

IX

VILLA SERBELLONI, BELLAGGIO

The fountain shivers lightly in the rain,
The laurels drip, the fading roses fall,
The marble satyr plays a mournful strain
That leaves the rainy fragrance musical.

Oh dripping laurel, Phœbus sacred tree,
Would that swift Daphne's lot might come to me,
Then would I still my soul and for an hour
Change to a laurel in the glancing shower.

X

The moon grows out of the hills
　A yellow flower,
The lake is a dreamy bride
　Who waits her hour.

Beauty has filled my heart,
　It can hold no more,
It is full, as the lake is full,
　From shore to shore.

XI

HAMBURG

The day that I come home,
　What will you find to say,—
Words as light as foam
　With laughter light as spray?

Yet say what words you will
　The day that I come home;
I shall hear the whole deep ocean
　Beating under the foam.

SAPPHO

I

Midnight, and in the darkness not a sound,
So, with hushed breathing, sleeps the autumn night;
Only the white immortal stars shall know,
Here in the house with the low-lintelled door,
How, for the last time, I have lit the lamp.
I think you are not wholly careless now,
Walls that have sheltered me so many an hour,
Bed that has brought me ecstasy and sleep,
Floors that have borne me when a gale of joy
Lifted my soul and made me half a god.
Farewell! Across the threshold many feet
Shall pass, but never Sappho's feet again.
Girls shall come in whom love has made aware
Of all their swaying beauty—they shall sing,
But never Sappho's voice, like golden fire,
Shall seek for heaven thru your echoing rafters.
There shall be swallows bringing back the spring
Over the long blue meadows of the sea,
And south-wind playing on the reeds of rain,
But never Sappho's whisper in the night,
Never her love-cry when the lover comes.
Farewell! I close the door and make it fast.

*   *   *   *   *   *

The little street lies meek beneath the moon,
Running, as rivers run, to meet the sea.
I too go seaward and shall not return.
Oh garlands on the doorposts that I pass,
Woven of asters and of autumn leaves,
I make a prayer for you: Cypris be kind,
That every lover may be given love.

I shall not hasten lest the paving stones
Should echo with my sandals and awake
Those who are warm beneath the cloak of sleep,
Lest they should rise and see me and should say,
"Whither goes Sappho lonely in the night?"
Whither goes Sappho? Whither all men go,
But they go driven, straining back with fear,
And Sappho goes as lightly as a leaf
Blown from brown autumn forests to the sea.

* * * * * *

Here on the rock Zeus lifted from the waves,
I shall await the waking of the dawn,
Lying beneath the weight of dark as one
Lies breathless, till the lover shall awake.
And with the sun the sea shall cover me—
I shall be less than the dissolving foam
Murmuring and melting on the ebbing tide;
I shall be less than spindrift, less than shells;
And yet I shall be greater than the gods,
For destiny no more can bow my soul
As rain bows down the watch-fires on the hills.
Yea, if my soul escape it shall aspire
To the white heaven as flame that has its will.
I go not bitterly, not dumb with pain,
Not broken by the ache of love—I go
As one grown tired lies down and hopes to sleep.
Yet they shall say: "It was for Cercolas;
She died because she could not bear her love."
They shall remember how we used to walk
Here on the cliff beneath the oleanders
In the long limpid twilight of the spring,
Looking toward Lemnos, where the amber sky
Was pierced with the faint arrow of a star.
How should they know the wind of a new beauty

Sweeping my soul had winnowed it with song?
I have been glad tho' love should come or go,
Happy as trees that find a wind to sway them,
Happy again when it has left them rest.
Others shall say, "Grave Dica wrought her death.
She would not lift her lips to take a kiss,
Or ever lift her eyes to take a smile.
She was a pool the winter paves with ice
That the wild hunter in the hills must leave
With thirst unslaked in the brief southward sun."
Ah Dica, it is not for thee I go;
And not for Phaon, tho' his ship lifts sail
Here in the windless harbor for the south.
Oh, darkling deities that guard the Nile,
Watch over one whose gods are far away.
Egypt, be kind to him, his eyes are deep—
Yet they are wrong who say it was for him.
How should they know that Sappho lived and died
Faithful to love, not faithful to the lover,
Never transfused and lost in what she loved,
Never so wholly loving nor at peace.
I asked for something greater than I found,
And every time that love has made me weep,
I have rejoiced that love could be so strong;
For I have stood apart and watched my soul
Caught in the gust of passion, as a bird
With baffled wings against the dusty whirlwind
Struggles and frees itself to find the sky.
It is not for a single god I go;
I have grown weary of the winds of heaven.
I will not be a reed to hold the sound
Of whatsoever breath the gods may blow,
Turning my torment into music for them.
They gave me life; the gift was bountiful,

I lived with the swift singing strength of fire,
Seeking for beauty as a flame for fuel—
Beauty in all things and in every hour.
The gods have given life—I gave them song;
The debt is paid and now I turn to go.

*   *   *   *   *   *

The breath of dawn blows the stars out like lamps,
There is a rim of silver on the sea,
As one grown tired who hopes to sleep, I go.

II

Oh Litis, little slave, why will you sleep?
These long Egyptian noons bend down your head
Bowed like the yarrow with a yellow bee.
There, lift your eyes no man has ever kindled,
Dark eyes that wait like faggots for the fire.
See how the temple's solid square of shade
Points north to Lesbos, and the splendid sea
That you have never seen, oh evening-eyed.
Yet have you never wondered what the Nile
Is seeking always, restless and wild with spring
And no less in the winter, seeking still?
How shall I tell you? Can you think of fields
Greater than Gods could till, more blue than night
Sown over with the stars; and delicate
With filmy nets of foam that come and go?
It is more cruel and more compassionate
Than harried earth. It takes with unconcern
And quick forgetting, rapture of the rain
And agony of thunder, the moon's white
Soft-garmented virginity, and then
The insatiable ardor of the sun.

· · 106 · ·

And me it took. But there is one more strong,
Love, that came laughing from the elder seas,
The Cyprian, the mother of the world;
She gave me love who only asked for death—
I who had seen much sorrow in men's eyes
And in my own too sorrowful a fire.
I was a sister of the stars, and yet
Shaken with pain; sister of birds and yet
The wings that bore my soul were very tired.
I watched the careless spring too many times
Light her green torches in a hungry wind;
Too many times I watched them flare, and then
Fall to forsaken embers in the autumn.
And I was sick of all things—even song.
In the dull autumn dawn I turned to death,
Buried my living body in the sea,
The strong cold sea that takes and does not give—
But there is one more strong, the Cyprian.
Litis, to wake from sleep and find your eyes
Met in their first fresh upward gaze by love,
Filled with love's happy shame from other eyes,
Dazzled with tenderness and drowned in light
As tho' you looked unthinking at the sun,
Oh Litis, that is joy! But if you came
Not from the sunny shallow pool of sleep,
But from the sea of death, the strangling sea
Of night and nothingness, and waked to find
Love looking down upon you, glad and still,
Strange and yet known forever, that is peace.
So did he lean above me. Not a word
He spoke; I only heard the morning sea
Singing against his happy ship, the keen
And straining joy of wind-awakened sails
And songs of mariners, and in myself

The precious pain of arms that held me fast.
They warmed the cold sea out of all my blood;
I slept, feeling his eyes above my sleep.
There on the ship with wines and olives laden,
Led by the stars to far invisible ports,
Egypt and islands of the inner seas,
Love came to me, and Cercolas was love.

III

The twilight's inner flame grows blue and deep,
And in my Lesbos, over leagues of sea,
The temples glimmer moon-wise in the trees.
Twilight has veiled the little flower-face
Here on my heart, but still the night is kind
And leaves her warm sweet weight against my breast.
Am I that Sappho who would run at dusk
Along the surges creeping up the shore
When tides came in to ease the hungry beach,
And running, running till the night was black,
Would fall forespent upon the chilly sand
And quiver with the winds from off the sea?
Ah quietly the shingle waits the tides
Whose waves are stinging kisses, but to me
Love brought no peace, nor darkness any rest.
I crept and touched the foam with fevered hands
And cried to Love, from whom the sea is sweet,
From whom the sea is bitterer than death.
Ah, Aphrodite, if I sing no more
To thee, God's daughter, powerful as God,
It is that thou hast made my life too sweet
To hold the added sweetness of a song.
There is a quiet at the heart of love,
And I have pierced the pain and come to peace.

I hold my peace, my Cleïs, on my heart;
And softer than a little wild bird's wing
Are kisses that she pours upon my mouth.
Ah never any more when spring like fire
Will flicker in the newly opened leaves,
Shall I steal forth to seek for solitude
Beyond the lure of light Alcæus' lyre,
Beyond the sob that stilled Erinna's voice.
Ah, never with a throat that aches with song,
Beneath the white uncaring sky of spring,
Shall I go forth to hide awhile from Love
The quiver and the crying of my heart.
Still I remember how I strove to flee
The love-note of the birds, and bowed my head
To hurry faster, but upon the ground
I saw two wingèd shadows side by side,
And all the world's spring passion stifled me.
Ah, Love, there is no fleeing from thy might,
No lonely place where thou hast never trod,
No desert thou hast left uncarpeted
With flowers that spring beneath thy perfect feet.
In many guises didst thou come to me;
I saw thee by the maidens while they danced,
Phaon allured me with a look of thine,
In Anactoria I knew thy grace,
I looked at Cercolas and saw thine eyes;
But never wholly, soul and body mine,
Didst thou bid any love me as I loved.
Now have I found the peace that fled from me;
Close, close against my heart I hold my world.
Ah, Love that made my life a lyric cry,
Ah, Love that tuned my lips to lyres of thine,
I taught the world thy music, now alone
I sing for one who falls asleep to hear.

Love Songs
(1917)

TO E.

I have remembered beauty in the night,
  Against black silences I waked to see
  A shower of sunlight over Italy
And green Ravello dreaming on her height;
I have remembered music in the dark,
  The clean swift brightness of a fugue of Bach's,
  And running water singing on the rocks
When once in English woods I heard a lark.

But all remembered beauty is no more
  Thank a vague prelude to the thought of you—
  You are the rarest soul I ever knew,
    Lover of beauty, knightliest and best;
My thoughts seek you as waves that seek the shore,
    And when I think of you, I am at rest.

I

BARTER

Life has loveliness to sell,
    All beautiful and splendid things,
Blue waves whitened on a cliff,
    Soaring fire that sways and sings,
And children's faces looking up
Holding wonder like a cup.

Life has loveliness to sell,
    Music like a curve of gold,
Scent of pine trees in the rain,
    Eyes that love you, arms that hold,
And for your spirit's still delight,
Holy thoughts that star the night.

Spend all you have for loveliness,
    Buy it and never count the cost;
For one white singing hour of peace
    Count many a year of strife well lost,
And for a breath of ecstasy
Give all you have been, or could be.

CHILD, CHILD

Child, child, love while you can
The voice and the eyes and the soul of a man;
Never fear though it break your heart—
Out of the wound new joy will start;
Only love proudly and gladly and well,
Though love be heaven or love be hell.

Child, child, love while you may,
For life is short as a happy day;
Never fear the thing you feel—
Only by love is life made real;
Love, for the deadly sins are seven,
Only through love will you enter heaven.

THE FOUNTAIN

All through the deep blue night
  The fountain sang alone;
It sang to the drowsy heart
  Of the satyr carved in stone.

The fountain sang and sang,
  But the satyr never stirred—
Only the great white moon
  In the empty heaven heard.

The fountain sang and sang
  While on the marble rim
The milk-white peacocks slept,
  And their dreams were strange and dim.

Bright dew was on the grass,
  And on the ilex, dew,
The dreamy milk-white birds
  Were all a-glisten, too.

The fountain sang and sang
  The things one cannot tell;
The dreaming peacocks stirred
  And the gleaming dew-drops fell.

TIDES

Love in my heart was a fresh tide flowing
    Where the starlike sea gulls soar;
The sun was keen and the foam was blowing
    High on the rocky shore.

But now in the dusk the tide is turning,
    Lower the sea gulls soar,
And the waves that rose in resistless yearning
    Are broken forevermore.

SPRING RAIN

I thought I had forgotten,
    But it all came back again
To-night with the first spring thunder
    In a rush of rain.

I remembered a darkened doorway
    Where we stood while the storm swept by,
Thunder gripping the earth
    And lightning scrawled on the sky.

The passing motor busses swayed,
    For the street was a river of rain,
Lashed into little golden waves
    In the lamp light's stain.

With the wild spring rain and thunder
    My heart was wild and gay;
Your eyes said more to me that night
    Than your lips would ever say. . . .

I thought I had forgotten,
　But it all came back again
To-night with the first spring thunder
　In a rush of rain.

JEWELS

If I should see your eyes again,
　I know how far their look would go—
Back to a morning in the park
　With sapphire shadows on the snow.

Or back to oak trees in the spring
　When you unloosed my hair and kissed
The head that lay against your knees
　In the leaf shadow's amethyst.

And still another shining place
　We would remember—how the dun
Wild mountain held us on its crest
　One diamond morning white with sun.

But I will turn my eyes from you
　As women turn to put away
The jewels they have worn at night
　And cannot wear in sober day.

INTERLUDE
Songs Out of Sorrow

SPIRIT'S HOUSE

From naked stones of agony
I will build a house for me;
As a mason all alone
I will raise it, stone by stone,
And every stone where I have bled
Will show a sign of dusky red.
I have not gone the way in vain,
For I have good of all my pain;
My spirit's quiet house will be
Built of naked stones I trod
On roads where I lost sight of God.

MASTERY

I would not have a god come in
To shield me suddenly from sin,
And set my house of life to rights;
Nor angels with bright burning wings
Ordering my earthly thoughts and things;
Rather my own frail guttering lights
Wind blown and nearly beaten out;
Rather the terror of the nights
And long, sick groping after doubt;
Rather be lost than let my soul
Slip vaguely from my own control—
Of my own spirit let me be
In sole though feeble mastery.

III

LESSONS

Unless I learn to ask no help
   From any other soul but mine,
To seek no strength in waving reeds
   Nor shade beneath a straggling pine;
Unless I learn to look at Grief
   Unshrinking from her tear-blind eyes,
And take from Pleasure fearlessly
   Whatever gifts will make me wise—
Unless I learn these things on earth,
Why was I ever given birth?

IV

WISDOM

When I have ceased to break my wings
Against the faultiness of things,
And learned that compromises wait
Behind each hardly opened gate,
When I can look Life in the eyes,
Grown calm and very coldly wise,
Life will have given me the Truth,
And taken in exchange—my youth.

V

IN A BURYING GROUND

This is the spot where I will lie
  When life has had enough of me,
These are the grasses that will blow
  Above me like a living sea.

These gay old lilies will not shrink
  To draw their life from death of mine,
And I will give my body's fire
  To make blue flowers on this vine.

"O Soul," I said, "have you no tears?
  Was not the body dear to you?"
I heard my soul say carelessly,
  "The myrtle flowers will grow more blue."

WOOD SONG

I heard a wood thrush in the dusk
  Twirl three notes and make a star—
My heart that walked with bitterness
  Came back from very far.

Three shining notes were all he had,
  And yet they made a starry call—
I caught life back against my breast
  And kissed it, scars and all.

· · 123 · ·

REFUGE

From my spirit's gray defeat,
From my pulse's flagging beat,
From my hopes that turned to sand
Sifting through my close-clenched hand,
From my own fault's slavery,
If I can sing, I still am free.

For with my singing I can make
A refuge for my spirit's sake,
A house of shining words, to be
My fragile immortality.

DEW

As dew leaves the cobweb lightly
   Threaded with stars,
Scattering jewels on the fence
   And the pasture bars;
As dawn leaves the dry grass bright
   And the tangled weeds
Bearing a rainbow gem
   On each of their seeds;
So has your love, my lover,
   Fresh as the dawn,
Made me a shining road
   To travel on,
Set every common sight
   Of tree or stone
Delicately alight
   For me alone.

TO-NIGHT

The moon is a curving flower of gold,
   The sky is still and blue;
The moon was made for the sky to hold,
   And I for you.

The moon is a flower without a stem,
   The sky is luminous;
Eternity was made for them,
   To-night for us.

BECAUSE

Oh, because you never tried
To bow my will or break my pride,
And nothing of the cave-man made
You want to keep me half afraid,
Nor ever with a conquering air
You thought to draw me unaware—
Take me, for I love you more
Than I ever loved before.

And since the body's maidenhood
Alone were neither rare nor good
Unless with it I gave to you
A spirit still untrammeled, too,
Take my dreams and take my mind
That were masterless as wind;
And "Master!" I shall say to you
Since you never asked me to.

THE TREE OF SONG

I sang my songs for the rest,
  For you I am still;
The tree of my song is bare
  On its shining hill.

For you came like a lordly wind,
  And the leaves were whirled
Far as forgotten things
  Past the rim of the world.

The tree of my song stands bare
  Against the blue—
I gave my songs to the rest,
  Myself to you.

RICHES

I have no riches but my thoughts,
  Yet these are wealth enough for me;
My thoughts of you are golden coins
  Stamped in the mint of memory;

And I must spend them all in song,
  For thoughts, as well as gold, must be
Left on the hither side of death
  To gain their immortality.

HOUSES OF DREAMS

You took my empty dreams
  And filled them every one
With tenderness and nobleness,
  April and the sun.

The old empty dreams
  Where my thoughts would throng
Are far too full of happiness
  To even hold a song.

Oh, the empty dreams were dim
  And the empty dreams were wide,
They were sweet and shadowy houses
  Where my thoughts could hide.

But you took my dreams away
　　And you made them all come true—
My thoughts have no place now to play,
　　And nothing now to do.

LIGHTS

When we come home at night and close the door,
　　Standing together in the shadowy room,
　　Safe in our own love and the gentle gloom,
Glad of familiar wall and chair and floor,

Glad to leave far below the clanging city;
　　Looking far downward to the glaring street
　　Gaudy with light, yet tired with many feet
In both of us wells up a wordless pity;

Men have tried hard to put away the dark;
　　A million lighted windows brilliantly
　　　　Inlay with squares of gold the winter night,
But to us standing here there comes the stark
　　　　Sense of the lives behind each yellow light,
　　And not one wholly joyous, proud, or free.

DOUBT

My soul lives in my body's house,
　　And you have both the house and her—
But sometimes she is less your own
　　Than a wild, gay adventurer;
A restless and an eager wraith,
　　How can I tell what she will do—
Oh, I am sure of my body's faith,
　　But what if my soul broke faith with you?

THE LAMP

If I can bear your love like a lamp before me,
When I go down the long steep Road of Darkness,
I shall not fear the everlasting shadows,
      Nor cry in terror.

If I can find out God, then I shall find Him,
If none can find Him, then I shall sleep soundly,
Knowing how well on earth your love sufficed me,
      A lamp in darkness.

IV

There! See the line of lights,
A chain of stars down either side the street—
Why can't you lift the chain and give it to me,
A necklace for my throat? I'd twist it round
And you could play with it. You smile at me
As though I were a little dreamy child
Behind whose eyes the fairies live. . . . And see,
The people on the street look up at us
All envious. We are a king and queen,
Our royal carriage is a motor bus,
We watch our subjects with a haughty joy. . . .
How still you are! Have you been hard at work
And are you tired to-night? It is so long
Since I have seen you—four whole days, I think.
My heart is crowded full of foolish thoughts
Like early flowers in an April meadow,
And I must give them to you, all of them,
Before they fade. The people I have met,
The play I saw, the trivial, shifting things
That loom too big or shrink too little, shadows
That hurry, gesturing along a wall,
Haunting or gay—and yet they all grow real
And take their proper size here in my heart
When you have seen them. . . . There's the Plaza now,
A lake of light! To-night it almost seems
That all the lights are gathered in your eyes,
Drawn somehow toward you. See the open park
Lying below us with a million lamps
Scattered in wise disorder like the stars.
We look down on them as God must look down
On constellations floating under Him
Tangled in clouds. . . . Come, then, and let us walk

Since we have reached the park. It is our garden,
All black and blossomless this winter night,
But we bring April with us, you and I;
We set the whole world on the trail of spring.
I think that every path we ever took
Has marked our footprints in mysterious fire,
Delicate gold that only fairies see.
When they wake up at dawn in hollow tree-trunks
And come out on the drowsy park, they look
Along the empty paths and say, "Oh, here
They went, and here, and here, and here! Come, see,
Here is their bench, take hands and let us dance
About it in a windy ring and make
A circle round it only they can cross
When they come back again!" . . . Look at the lake—
Do you remember how we watched the swans
That night in late October while they slept?
Swans must have stately dreams, I think. But now
The lake bears only thin reflected lights
That shake a little. How I long to take
One from the cold black water—new-made gold
To give you in your hand! And see, and see,
There is a star, deep in the lake, a star!
Oh, dimmer than a pearl—if you stoop down
Your hand could almost reach it up to me. . . .

There was a new frail yellow moon to-night—
I wish you could have had it for a cup
With stars like dew to fill it to the brim. . . .

How cold it is! Even the lights are cold;
They have put shawls of fog around them, see!
What if the air should grow so dimly white
That we would lose our way along the paths

Made new by walls of moving mist receding
The more we follow. . . . What a silver night!
That was our bench the time you said to me
The long new poem—but how different now,
How eerie with the curtain of the fog
Making it strange to all the friendly trees!
There is no wind, and yet great curving scrolls
Carve themselves, ever changing, in the mist.
Walk on a little, let me stand here watching
To see you, too, grown strange to me and far. . . .

I used to wonder how the park would be
If one night we could have it all alone—
No lovers with close arm-encircled waists
To whisper and break in upon our dreams.
And now we have it! Every wish comes true!
We are alone now in a fleecy world;
Even the stars have gone. We two alone!

Flame and Shadow

(1920)

BLUE SQUILLS

How many million Aprils came
   Before I ever knew
How white a cherry bough could be,
   A bed of squills, how blue!

And many a dancing April
   When life is done with me,
Will lift the blue flame of the flower
   And the white flame of the tree.

Oh burn me with your beauty, then,
   Oh hurt me, tree and flower,
Lest in the end death try to take
   Even this glistening hour.

O shaken flowers, O shimmering trees,
   O sunlit white and blue,
Wound me, that I, through endless sleep,
   May bear the scar of you.

STARS

Alone in the night
   On a dark hill
With pines around me
   Spicy and still,

And a heaven full of stars
   Over my head,
White and topaz
   And misty red;

Myriads with beating
    Hearts of fire
That aeons
    Cannot vex or tire;

Up the dome of heaven
    Like a great hill,
I watch them marching
    Stately and still,

And I know that I
    Am honored to be
Witness
    Of so much majesty.

"WHAT DO I CARE?"

What do I care, in the dreams and the languor of spring,
    That my songs do not show me at all?
For they are a fragrance, and I am a flint and a fire,
    I am an answer, they are only a call.

But what do I care, for love will be over so soon,
    Let my heart have its say and my mind stand idly by,
For my mind is proud and strong enough to be silent,
    It is my heart that makes my songs, not I.

MEADOWLARKS

In the silver light after a storm,
    Under dripping boughs of bright new green,
I take the low path to hear the meadowlarks
    Alone and high-hearted as if I were a queen.

What have I to fear in life or death
  Who have known three things: the kiss in the night,
The white flying joy when a song is born,
  And meadowlarks whistling in silver light.

DRIFTWOOD

My forefathers gave me
  My spirit's shaken flame,
The shape of hands, the beat of heart,
  The letters of my name.

But it was my lovers,
  And not my sleeping sires,
Who gave the flame its changeful
  And iridescent fires;

As the driftwood burning
  Learned its jewelled blaze
From the sea's blue splendor
  Of colored nights and days.

"I HAVE LOVED HOURS AT SEA"

I have loved hours at sea, gray cities,
  The fragile secret of a flower,
Music, the making of a poem
  That gave me heaven for an hour;

First stars above a snowy hill,
  Voices of people kindly and wise,
And the great look of love, long hidden,
  Found at last in meeting eyes.

I have loved much and been loved deeply—
   Oh when my spirit's fire burns low,
Leave me the darkness and the stillness,
   I shall be tired and glad to go.

AUGUST MOONRISE

The sun was gone, and the moon was coming
Over the blue Connecticut hills;
The west was rosy, the east was flushed,
And over my head the swallows rushed
This way and that, with changeful wills.
I heard them twitter and watched them dart
Now together and now apart
Like dark petals blown from a tree;
The maples stamped against the west
Were black and stately and full of rest,
And the hazy orange moon grew up
And slowly changed to yellow gold
While the hills were darkened, fold on fold
To a deeper blue than a flower could hold.
Down the hill I went, and then
I forgot the ways of men,
For night-scents, heady, and damp and cool
Wakened ecstasy in me
On the brink of a shining pool.

O Beauty, out of many a cup
You have made me drunk and wild
Ever since I was a child,
But when have I been sure as now
That no bitterness can bend
And no sorrow wholly bow
One who loves you to the end?

And though I must give my breath
And my laughter all to death,
And my eyes through which joy came,
And my heart, a wavering flame;
If all must leave me and go back
Along a blind and fearful track
So that you can make anew,
Fusing with intenser fire,
Something nearer your desire;
If my soul must go alone
Through a cold infinity,
Or even if it vanish, too,
Beauty, I have worshipped you.

Let this single hour atone
For the theft of all of me

II

MEMORIES

PLACES

Places I love come back to me like music,
    Hush me and heal me when I am very tired;
I see the oak woods at Saxton's flaming
    In a flare of crimson by the frost newly fired;
And I am thirsty for the spring in the valley
    As for a kiss ungiven and long desired.

I know a bright world of snowy hills at Boonton,
    A blue and white dazzling light on everything one sees,
The ice-covered branches of the hemlocks sparkle
    Bending low and tinkling in the sharp thin breeze,
And iridescent crystals fall and crackle on the snow-crust
    With the winter sun drawing cold blue shadows from the
        trees.

Violet now, in veil on veil of evening,
    The hills across from Cromwell grow dreamy and far;
A wood-thrush is singing soft as a viol
    In the heart of the hollow where the dark pools are;
The primrose has opened her pale yellow flowers
    And heaven is lighting star after star.

Places I love come back to me like music—
    Mid-ocean, midnight, the waves buzz drowsily;
In the ship's deep churning the eerie phosphorescence
    Is like the souls of people who were drowned at sea,
And I can hear a man's voice, speaking, hushed, insistent,
    At midnight, in mid-ocean, hour on hour to me.

OLD TUNES

As the waves of perfume, heliotrope, rose,
Float in the garden when no wind blows,
Come to us, go from us, whence no one knows;

So the old tunes float in my mind,
And go from me leaving no trace behind,
Like fragrance borne on the hush of the wind.

But in the instant the airs remain
I know the laughter and the pain
Of times that will not come again.

I try to catch at many a tune
Like petals of light fallen from the moon,
Broken and bright on a dark lagoon,

But they float away—for who can hold
Youth, or perfume or the moon's gold?

"ONLY IN SLEEP"

Only in sleep I see their faces,
  Children I played with when I was a child,
Louise comes back with her brown hair braided,
  Annie with ringlets warm and wild.

Only in sleep Time is forgotten—
  What may have come to them, who can know?
  Yet we played last night as long ago,
And the doll-house stood at the turn of the stair.

The years had not sharpened their smooth round faces,
  I met their eyes and found them mild—
Do they, too, dream of me, I wonder,
  And for them am I, too, a child?

REDBIRDS

Redbirds, redbirds,
  Long and long ago,
What a honey-call you had
  In hills I used to know;

Redbud, buckberry,
  Wild plum-tree
And proud river sweeping
  Southward to the sea,

Brown and gold in the sun
  Sparkling far below,
Trailing stately round her bluffs
  Where the poplars grow——

Redbirds, redbirds,
  Are you singing still
As you sang one May day
  On Saxton's Hill?

SUNSET
(St. Louis)

Hushed in the smoky haze of summer sunset,
When I came home again from far-off places,
How many times I saw my western city
  Dream by her river.

Then for an hour the water wore a mantle
Of tawny gold and mauve and misted turquoise
Under the tall and darkened arches bearing
  Gray, high-flung bridges.

Against the sunset, water-towers and steeples
Flickered with fire up the slope to westward,
And old warehouses poured their purple shadows
    Across the levee.

High over them the black train swept with thunder,
Cleaving the city, leaving far beneath it
Wharf-boats moored beside the old side-wheelers
    Resting in twilight.

THE COIN

Into my heart's treasury
    I slipped a coin
That time cannot take
    Nor a thief purloin,—
Oh, better than the minting
    Of a gold-crowned king
Is the safe-kept memory
    Of a lovely thing.

THE VOICE

Atoms as old as stars,
Mutation on mutation,
Millions and millions of cells
Dividing yet still the same,
From air and changing earth,
From ancient Eastern rivers,
From turquoise tropic seas,
Unto myself I came.

My spirit like my flesh
Sprang from a thousand sources,
From cave-man, hunter and shepherd,
From Karnak, Cyprus, Rome;
The living thoughts in me
Spring from dead men and women,
Forgotten time out of mind
And many as bubbles of foam.

Here for a moment's space
Into the light out of darkness,
I come and they come with me
Finding words with my breath;
From the wisdom of many life-times
I hear them cry: "Forever
Seek for Beauty, she only
Fights with man against Death!"

III

DAY AND NIGHT

In Warsaw in Poland
    Half the world away,
The one I love best of all
    Thought of me to-day;

I know, for I went
    Winged as a bird,
In the wide flowing wind
    His own voice I heard;

His arms were round me
    In a ferny place,
I looked in the pool
    And there was his face—

But now it is night
    And the cold stars say:
"Warsaw in Poland
    Is half the world away."

COMPENSATION

I should be glad of loneliness
    And hours that go on broken wings,
A thirsty body, a tired heart
    And the unchanging ache of things,
If I could make a single song
    As lovely and as full of light,
As hushed and brief as a falling star
    On a winter night.

I REMEMBERED

There never was a mood of mine,
  Gay or heart-broken, luminous or dull,
But you could ease me of its fever
  And give it back to me more beautiful.

In many another soul I broke the bread,
  And drank the wine and played the happy guest,
But I was lonely, I remembered you;
  The heart belongs to him who knew it best.

GRAY EYES

It was April when you came
  The first time to me,
And my first look in your eyes
  Was like my first look at the sea.

We have been together
  Four Aprils now
Watching for the green
  On the swaying willow bough;

Yet whenever I turn
  To your gray eyes over me,
It is as though I looked
  For the first time at the sea.

THE NET

I made you many and many a song,
  Yet never one told all you are—
It was as though a net of words
  Were flung to catch a star;

It was as though I curved my hand
  And dipped sea-water eagerly,
Only to find it lost the blue
  Dark splendor of the sea.

THE MYSTERY

Your eyes drink of me,
  Love makes them shine,
Your eyes that lean
  So close to mine.

We have long been lovers,
  We know the range
Of each other's moods
  And how they change;

But when we look
  At each other so
Then we feel
  How little we know;

The spirit eludes us,
  Timid and free—
Can I ever know you
  Or you know me?

IV

IN A HOSPITAL

OPEN WINDOWS

Out of the window a sea of green trees
    Lift their soft boughs like the arms of a dancer,
They beckon and call me, "Come out in the sun!"
    But I cannot answer.

I am alone with Weakness and Pain,
    Sick abed and June is going,
I cannot keep her, she hurries by
    With the silver-green of her garments blowing.

Men and women pass in the street
    Glad of the shining sapphire weather,
But we know more of it than they,
    Pain and I together.

They are the runners in the sun,
    Breathless and blinded by the race,
But we are watchers in the shade
    Who speak with Wonder face to face.

THE NEW MOON

Day, you have bruised and beaten me,
As rain beats down the bright, proud sea,
Beaten my body, bruised my soul,
Left me nothing lovely or whole—
Yet I have wrested a gift from you,
Day that dies in dusky blue:

For suddenly over the factories
I saw a moon in the cloudy seas—
A wisp of beauty all alone
In a world as hard and gray as stone—
Oh who could be bitter and want to die
When a maiden moon wakes up in the sky?

LOST THINGS

Oh, I could let the world go by,
　　Its loud new wonders and its wars,
But how will I give up the sky
　　When winter dusk is set with stars?

And I could let the cities go,
　　Their changing customs and their creeds,—
But oh, the summer rains that blow
　　In silver on the jewel-weeds!

PAIN

Waves are the sea's white daughters,
　　And raindrops the children of rain,
But why for my shimmering body
　　Have I a mother like Pain?

Night is the mother of stars,
　　And wind the mother of foam—
The world is brimming with beauty,
　　But I must stay at home.

THE BROKEN FIELD

My soul is a dark ploughed field
   In the cold rain;
My soul is a broken field
   Ploughed by pain.

Where grass and bending flowers
   Were growing,
The field lies broken now
   For another sowing.

Great Sower when you tread
   My field again,
Scatter the furrows there
   With better grain.

THE UNSEEN

Death went up the hall
   Unseen by every one,
Trailing twilight robes
   Past the nurse and the nun.

He paused at every door
   And listened to the breath
Of those who did not know
   How near they were to Death.

Death went up the hall
   Unseen by nurse and nun;
He passed by many a door—
   But he entered one.

A PRAYER

When I am dying, let me know
That I loved the blowing snow
   Although it stung like whips;
That I loved all lovely things
And I tried to take their stings
   With gay unembittered lips;
That I loved with all my strength,
To my soul's full depth and length,
   Careless if my heart must break,
That I sang as children sing
Fitting tunes to everything,
   Loving life for its own sake.

V

SPRING TORRENTS

Will it always be like this until I am dead,
   Every spring must I bear it all again
With the first red haze of the budding maple boughs,
   And the first sweet-smelling rain?

Oh I am like a rock in the rising river
   Where the flooded water breaks with a low call—
Like a rock that knows the cry of the waters
   And cannot answer at all.

"I KNOW THE STARS"

I know the stars by their names,
   Aldebaran, Altair,
And I know the path they take
   Up heaven's broad blue stair.

I know the secrets of men
   By the look of their eyes,
Their gray thoughts, their strange thoughts
   Have made me sad and wise.

But your eyes are dark to me
   Though they seem to call and call—
I cannot tell if you love me
   Or do not love me at all.

I know many things,
   But the years come and go,
I shall die not knowing
   The thing I long to know.

UNDERSTANDING

I understood the rest too well,
    And all their thoughts have come to be
Clear as grey sea-weed in the swell
    Of a sunny shallow sea.

But you I never understood,
    Your spirit's secret hides like gold
Sunk in a Spanish galleon
    Ages ago in waters cold.

NIGHTFALL

We will never walk again
    As we used to walk at night,
Watching our shadows lengthen
    Under the gold street-light
    When the snow was new and white.

We will never walk again
    Slowly, we two,
In spring when the park is sweet
    With midnight and with dew,
    And the passers-by are few.

I sit and think of it all,
    And the blue June twilight dies,—
Down in the clanging square
    A street-piano cries
    And stars come out in the skies.

"IT IS NOT A WORD"

It is not a word spoken,
　　Few words are said;
Nor even a look of the eyes
　　Nor a bend of the head,
But only a hush of the heart
　　That has too much to keep,
Only memories waking
　　That sleep so light a sleep.

"MY HEART IS HEAVY"

My heart is heavy with many a song
　　Like ripe fruit bearing down the tree,
But I can never give you one—
　　My songs do not belong to me.

Yet in the evening, in the dusk
　　When moths go to and fro,
In the gray hour if the fruit has fallen,
　　Take it, no one will know.

THE NIGHTS REMEMBER

The days remember and the nights remember
　　The kingly hours that once you made so great,
Deep in my heart they lie, hidden in their splendor,
　　Buried like sovereigns in their robes of state.

Let them not wake again, better to lie there,
　　Wrapped in memories, jewelled and arrayed—
Many a ghostly king has waked from death-sleep
　　And found his crown stolen and his throne decayed.

"LET IT BE FORGOTTEN"

Let it be forgotten, as a flower is forgotten,
   Forgotten as a fire that once was singing gold,
Let it be forgotten for ever and ever,
   Time is a kind friend, he will make us old.

If anyone asks, say it was forgotten
   Long and long ago,
As a flower, as a fire, as a hushed footfall
   In a long forgotten snow.

VI

THE DARK CUP

A delicate fabric of bird song
   Floats in the air,
The smell of wet wild earth
   Is everywhere.

Red small leaves of the maple
   Are clenched like a hand,
Like girls at their first communion
   The pear trees stand.

Oh I must pass nothing by
   Without loving it much,
The raindrop try with my lips,
   The grass with my touch;

For how can I be sure
   I shall see again
The world on the first of May
   Shining after the rain?

"THE DREAMS OF MY HEART"

The dreams of my heart and my mind pass,
   Nothing stays with me long,
But I have had from a child
   The deep solace of song;

If that should ever leave me,
   Let me find death and stay
With things whose tunes are played out and forgotten
   Like the rain of yesterday.

"A LITTLE WHILE"

A little while when I am gone
  My life will live in music after me,
As spun foam lifted and borne on
  After the wave is lost in the full sea.

A while these nights and days will burn
  In song with the bright frailty of foam,
Living in light before they turn
  Back to the nothingness that is their home.

THE GARDEN

My heart is a garden tired with autumn,
  Heaped with bending asters and dahlias heavy and dark,
In the hazy sunshine, the garden remembers April,
  The drench of rains and a snow-drop quick and clear as a
    spark;

Daffodils blowing in the cold wind of morning,
  And golden tulips, goblets holding the rain—
The garden will be hushed with snow, forgotten soon, for-
    gotten—
  After the stillness, will spring come again?

THE WINE

I cannot die, who drank delight
  From the cup of the crescent moon,
And hungrily as men eat bread,
  Loved the scented nights of June.

The rest may die—but is there not
    Some shining strange escape for me
Who sought in Beauty the bright wine
    Of immortality?

IN A CUBAN GARDEN

Hibiscus flowers are cups of fire,
    (Love me, my lover, life will not stay)
The bright poinsettia shakes in the wind,
    A scarlet leaf is blowing away.

A lizard lifts his head and listens—
    Kiss me before the noon goes by,
Here in the shade of the ceiba hide me
    From the great black vulture circling the sky.

"IF I MUST GO"

If I must go to heaven's end
    Climbing the ages like a stair,
Be near me and forever bend
    With the same eyes above me there;
Time will fly past us like leaves flying,
    We shall not heed, for we shall be
Beyond living, beyond dying,
    Knowing and known unchangeably.

IN SPRING, SANTA BARBARA

I have been happy two weeks together,
   My love is coming home to me,
Gold and silver is the weather
   And smooth as lapis is the sea.

The earth has turned its brown to green
   After three nights of humming rain,
And in the valleys peck and preen
   Linnets with a scarlet stain.

High in the mountains all alone
   The wild swans whistle on the lakes,
But I have been as still as stone,
   My heart sings only when it breaks.

WHITE FOG

Heaven-invading hills are drowned
   In wide moving waves of mist,
Phlox before my door are wound
   In dripping wreaths of amethyst.

Ten feet away the solid earth
   Changes into melting cloud,
There is a hush of pain and mirth,
   No bird has heart to speak aloud.

Here in a world without a sky,
   Without the ground, without the sea,
The one unchanging thing is I,
   Myself remains to comfort me.

ARCTURUS

Arcturus brings the spring back
   As surely now as when
He rose on eastern islands
   For Grecian girls and men;

The twilight is as clear a blue,
   The star as shaken and as bright,
And the same thought he gave to them
   He gives to me to-night.

MOONLIGHT

It will not hurt me when I am old,
   A running tide where moonlight burned
     Will not sting me like silver snakes;
The years will make me sad and cold,
     It is the happy heart that breaks.

The heart asks more than life can give,
   When that is learned, then all is learned;
     The waves break fold on jewelled fold,
But beauty itself is fugitive,
     It will not hurt me when I am old.

MORNING SONG

A diamond of a morning
   Waked me an hour too soon;
Dawn had taken in the stars
   And left the faint white moon.

O white moon, you are lonely,
    It is the same with me,
But we have the world to roam **over,**
    Only the lonely are free.

GRAY FOG

A fog drifts in, the heavy laden
    Cold white ghost of the sea—
One by one the hills go out,
    The road and the pepper-tree.

I watch the fog float in at the window
    With the whole world gone blind,
Everything, even my longing, drowses,
    Even the thoughts in my mind.

I put my head on my hands before me,
    There is nothing left to be done or said,
There is nothing to hope for, I am tired,
    And heavy as the dead.

BELLS

At six o'clock of an autumn dusk
    With the sky in the west a rusty red,
The bells of the mission down in the valley
    Cry out that the day is dead.

The first star pricks as sharp as steel—
    Why am I suddenly so cold?
Three bells, each with a separate sound
    Clang in the valley, wearily tolled.

Bells in Venice, bells at sea,
   Bells in the valley heavy and slow—
There is no place over the crowded world
   Where I can forget that the days go.

LOVELY CHANCE

O lovely chance, what can I do
To give my gratefulness to you?
You rise between myself and me
With a wise persistency;
I would have broken body and soul,
But by your grace, still I am whole.
Many a thing you did to save me,
Many a holy gift you gave me,
Music and friends and happy love
More than my dearest dreaming of;
And now in this wide twilight hour
With earth and heaven a dark, blue flower,
In a humble mood I bless
Your wisdom—and your waywardness.
You brought me even here, where I
Live on a hill against the sky
And look on mountains and the sea
And a thin white moon in the pepper tree.

VIII

"THERE WILL COME SOFT RAINS"

(War Time)

There will come soft rains and the smell of the ground,
And swallows circling with their shimmering sound;

And frogs in the pools singing at night,
And wild plum-trees in tremulous white;

Robins will wear their feathery fire
Whistling their whims on a low fence-wire;

And not one will know of the war, not one
Will care at last when it is done.

Not one would mind, neither bird nor tree
If mankind perished utterly;

And Spring herself, when she woke at dawn,
Would scarcely know that we were gone.

NAHANT

Bowed as an elm under the weight of its beauty,
So earth is bowed, under her weight of splendor,
Molten sea, richness of leaves and the burnished
   Bronze of sea-grasses.

Clefts in the cliff shelter the purple sand-peas
And chicory flowers bluer than the ocean
Flinging its foam high, white fire in sunshine,
   Jewels of water.

Joyous thunder of blown waves on the ledges,
Make me forget war and the dark war-sorrow—
Against the sky a sentry paces the sea-cliff
  Slim in his khaki.

A BOY

Out of the noise of tired people working,
  Harried with thoughts of war and lists of dead,
His beauty met me like a fresh wind blowing,
  Clean boyish beauty and high-held head.

Eyes that told secrets, lips that would not tell them,
  Fearless and shy the young unwearied eyes—
Men die by millions now, because God blunders,
  Yet to have made this boy he must be wise.

IX

BY THE SEA

THE UNCHANGING

Sun-swept beaches with a light wind blowing
  From the immense blue circle of the sea,
And the soft thunder where long waves whiten—
  These were the same for Sappho as for me.

Two thousand years—much has gone by forever,
Change takes the gods and ships and speech of men—
But here on the beaches that time passes over
  The heart aches now as then.

JUNE NIGHT

Oh Earth, you are too dear to-night,
  How can I sleep while all around
Floats rainy fragrance and the far
  Deep voice of the ocean that talks to the ground?

Oh Earth, you gave me all I have,
  I love you, I love you,—oh what have I
That I can give you in return—
  Except my body after I die?

"LIKE BARLEY BENDING"

Like barley bending
  In low fields by the sea,
Singing in hard wind
  Ceaselessly;

Like barley bending
  And rising again,
So would I, unbroken,
  Rise from pain;

So would I softly,
  Day long, night long,
Change my sorrow
  Into song.

"OH DAY OF FIRE AND SUN"

Oh day of fire and sun,
  Pure as a naked flame,
Blue sea, blue sky and dun
  Sands where he spoke my name;

Laughter and hearts so high
  That the spirit flew off free,
Lifting into the sky
  Diving into the sea;

Oh day of fire and sun
  Like a crystal burning,
Slow days go one by one,
  But you have no returning.

"I THOUGHT OF YOU"

I thought of you and how you love this beauty,
  And walking up the long beach all alone
I heard the waves breaking in measured thunder
  As you and I once heard their monotone.

Around me were the echoing dunes, beyond me
   The cold and sparkling silver of the sea—
We two will pass through death and ages lengthen
   Before you hear that sound again with me.

ON THE DUNES

If there is any life when death is over,
   These tawny beaches will know much of me,
I shall come back, as constant and as changeful
   As the unchanging, many-colored sea.

If life was small, if it has made me scornful,
   Forgive me; I shall straighten like a flame
In the great calm of death, and if you want me
   Stand on the sea-ward dunes and call my name.

SPRAY

I knew you thought of me all night,
   I knew, though you were far away;
     I felt your love blow over me
     As if a dark wind-riven sea
Drenched me with quivering spray.

There are so many ways to love
   And each way has its own delight—
     Then be content to come to me
     Only as spray the beating sea
Drives inland through the night.

IF DEATH IS KIND

Perhaps if Death is kind, and there can be returning,
   We will come back to earth some fragrant night,
And take these lanes to find the sea, and bending
   Breathe the same honeysuckle, low and white.

We will come down at night to these resounding beaches
   And the long gentle thunder of the sea,
Here for a single hour in the wide starlight
   We shall be happy, for the dead are free.

X

THOUGHTS

When I am all alone
  Envy me most,
Then my thoughts flutter round me
  In a glimmering host;

Some dressed in silver,
  Some dressed in white,
Each like a taper
  Blossoming light;

Most of them merry,
  Some of them grave,
Each of them lithe
  As willows that wave;

Some bearing violets,
  Some bearing bay,
One with a burning rose
  Hidden away—

When I am all alone
  Envy me then,
For I have better friends
  Than women and men.

FACES

People that I meet and pass
  In the city's broken roar,
Faces that I lose so soon
  And have never found before,

Do you know how much you tell
    In the meeting of our eyes,
How ashamed I am, and sad
    To have pierced your poor disguise?

Secrets rushing without sound
    Crying from your hiding places—
Let me go, I cannot bear
    The sorrow of the passing faces.

—People in the restless street,
    Can it be, oh can it be
In the meeting of our eyes
    That you know as much of me?

EVENING

(New York)

Blue dust of evening over my city,
    Over the ocean of roofs and the tall towers
Where the window-lights, myriads and myriads,
    Bloom from the walls like climbing flowers.

SNOWFALL

"She can't be unhappy," you said,
    "The smiles are like stars in her eyes,
And her laugh is thistledown
    Around her low replies."
"Is she unhappy?" you said—
    But who has ever known
Another's heartbreak—
    All he can know is his own;

And she seems hushed to me,
    As hushed as though
Her heart were a hunter's fire
    Smothered in snow.

THE SANCTUARY

If I could keep my innermost Me
Fearless, aloof and free
Of the least breath of love or hate,
And not disconsolate
At the sick load of sorrow laid on men;
If I could keep a sanctuary there
Free even of prayer,
If I could do this, then,
With quiet candor as I grew more wise
I could look even at God with grave forgiving eyes.

AT SEA

In the pull of the wind I stand, lonely,
    On the deck of a ship, rising, falling,
Wild night around me, wild water under me,
    Whipped by the storm, screaming and calling.

Earth is hostile and the sea hostile,
    Why do I look for a place to rest?
I must fight always and die fighting
    With fear an unhealing wound in my breast.

DUST

When I went to look at what had long been hidden,
  A jewel laid long ago in a secret place,
I trembled, for I thought to see its dark deep fire—
  But only a pinch of dust blew up in my face.

I almost gave my life long ago for a thing
  That has gone to dust now, stinging my eyes—
It is strange how often a heart must be broken
  Before the years can make it wise.

THE LONG HILL

I must have passed the crest a while ago
  And now I am going down—
Strange to have crossed the crest and not to know,
  But the brambles were always catching the hem of my
    gown.

All the morning I thought how proud I should be
  To stand there straight as a queen,
Wrapped in the wind and the sun with the world under me—
  But the air was dull, there was little I could have seen.

It was nearly level along the beaten track
  And the brambles caught in my gown—
But it's no use now to think of turning back,
  The rest of the way will be only going down.

XI

IN THE END

All that could never be said,
   All that could never be done,
Wait for us at last
   Somewhere back of the sun;

All the heart broke to forego
   Shall be ours without pain,
We shall take them as lightly as girls
   Pluck flowers after rain.

And when they are ours in the end
   Perhaps after all
The skies will not open for us
   Nor heaven be there at our call.

"IT WILL NOT CHANGE"

It will not change now
   After so many years;
Life has not broken it
   With parting or tears;
Death will not alter it,
   It will live on
In all my songs for you
   When I am gone.

CHANGE

Remember me as I was then;
   Turn from me now, but always see
The laughing shadowy girl who stood
   At midnight by the flowering tree,
With eyes that love had made as bright
As the trembling stars of the summer night

Turn from me now, but always hear
   The muted laughter in the dew
Of that one year of youth we had,
   The only youth we ever knew—
Turn from me now, or you will see
What other years have done to me.

WATER LILIES

If you have forgotten water lilies floating
   On a dark lake among mountains in the afternoon shade,
If you have forgotten their wet, sleepy fragrance,
   Then you can return and not be afraid.

But if you remember, then turn away forever
   To the plains and the prairies where pools are far apart,
There you will not come at dusk on closing water lilies,
   And the shadow of mountains will not fall on your heart.

THE STORM

I thought of you when I was wakened
　　By a wind that made me glad and afraid
Of the rushing, pouring sound of the sea
　　That the great trees made.

One thought in my mind went over and over
　　While the darkness shook and the leaves
　　　　were thinned—
I thought it was you who had come to find me,
　　You were the wind.

XII

SONGS FOR MYSELF

THE TREE

Oh to be free of myself,
　With nothing left to remember,
To have my heart as bare
　As a tree in December;

Resting, as a tree rests
　After its leaves are gone,
Waiting no more for a rain at night
　Nor for the red at dawn;

But still, oh so still
　While the winds come and go,
With no more fear of the hard frost
　Or the bright burden of snow;

And heedless, heedless
　If anyone pass and see
On the white page of the sky
　Its thin black tracery.

AT MIDNIGHT

Now at last I have come to see what life is,
　Nothing is ever ended, everything only begun,
And the brave victories that seem so splendid
　Are never really won.

Even love that I built my spirit's house for,
　Comes like a brooding and a baffled guest,
And music and men's praise and even laughter
　Are not so good as rest.

SONG MAKING

My heart cried like a beaten child
    Ceaselessly all night long;
I had to take my own cries
    And thread them into a song.

One was a cry at black midnight
    And one when the first cock crew—
My heart was like a beaten child,
    But no one ever knew.

Life, you have put me in your debt
    And I must serve you long—
But oh, the debt is terrible
    That must be paid in song.

ALONE

I am alone, in spite of love,
    In spite of all I take and give—
In spite of all your tenderness,
    Sometimes I am not glad to live.

I am alone, as though I stood
    On the highest peak of the tired gray world,
About me only swirling snow,
    Above me endless space unfurled;

With earth hidden and heaven hidden,
    And only my own spirit's pride
To keep me from the peace of those
    Who are not lonely, having died.

RED MAPLES

In the last year I have learned
How few men are worth my trust;
I have seen the friend I loved
Struck by death into the dust,
And fears I never knew before
Have knocked and knocked upon my door—
"I shall hope little and ask for less,"
I said, "There is no happiness."

I have grown wise at last—but how
Can I hide the gleam on the willow-bough,
Or keep the fragrance out of the rain
Now that April is here again?
When maples stand in a haze of fire
What can I say to the old desire,
What shall I do with the joy in me
That is born out of agony?

DEBTOR

So long as my spirit still
　　Is glad of breath
And lifts its plumes of pride
　　In the dark face of death;
While I am curious still
　　Of love and fame,
Keeping my heart too high
　　For the years to tame,
How can I quarrel with fate
　　Since I can see
I am a debtor to life,
　　Not life to me?

THE WIND IN THE HEMLOCK

Steely stars and moon of brass,
How mockingly you watch me pass!
You know as well as I how soon
I shall be blind to stars and moon,
Deaf to the wind in the hemlock tree,
Dumb when the brown earth weighs on me.

With envious dark rage I bear,
Stars, your cold complacent stare;
Heart-broken in my hate look up,
Moon, at your clear immortal cup,
Changing to gold from dusky red—
Age after age when I am dead
To be filled up with light, and then
Emptied, to be refilled again.
What has man done that only he
Is slave to death—so brutally
Beaten back into the earth
Impatient for him since his birth?

Oh let me shut my eyes, close out
The sight of stars and earth and be
Sheltered a minute by this tree.
Hemlock, through your fragrant boughs
There moves no anger and no doubt,
No envy of immortal things.
The night-wind murmurs of the sea
With veiled music ceaselessly,
That to my shaken spirit sings.
From their frail nest the robins rouse,
In your pungent darkness stirred,

Twittering a low drowsy word—
And me you shelter, even me.
In your quietness you house
The wind, the woman and the bird.
You speak to me and I have heard:

If I am peaceful, I shall see
Beauty's face continually;
Feeding on her wine and bread
I shall be wholly comforted,
For she can make one day for me
Rich as my lost eternity.

Dark of the Moon
(1926)

I

THERE WILL BE STARS

ON THE SUSSEX DOWNS

Over the downs there were birds flying,
  Far off glittered the sea,
And toward the north the weald of Sussex
  Lay like a kingdom under me.

I was happier than the larks
  That nest on the downs and sing to the sky,
Over the downs the birds flying
  Were not so happy as I.

It was not you, though you were near,
  Though you were good to hear and see,
It was not earth, it was not heaven
  It was myself that sang in me.

AUGUST NIGHT

On a midsummer night, on a night that was eerie with stars,
  In a wood too deep for a single star to look through,
You led down a path whose turnings you knew in the dark-
      ness,
  But the scent of the dew-dripping cedars was all that I
      knew.

I drank of the darkness, I was fed with the honey of fragrance,
  I was glad of my life, the drawing of breath was sweet;
I heard your voice, you said, "Look down, see the glow-worm!"
  It was there before me, a small star white at my feet.

We watched while it brightened as though it were breathed
    on and burning,
  This tiny creature moving over earth's floor—
" '*L'amor che move il sole e l'altre stelle*,"
  You said, and no more.

TWO MINDS

Your mind and mine are such great lovers they
Have freed themselves from cautious human clay,
And on wild clouds of thought, naked together
They ride above us in extreme delight;
We see them, we look up with a lone envy
And watch them in their zone of crystal weather
That changes not for winter or the night.

WORDS FOR AN OLD AIR

Your heart is bound tightly, let
  Beauty beware,
It is not hers to set
  Free from the snare.

Tell her a bleeding hand
  Bound it and tied it,
Tell her the knot will stand
  Though she deride it;

One who withheld so long
  All that you yearned to take,
Has made a snare too strong
  For Beauty's self to break.

· · 222 · ·

MOUNTAIN WATER

You have taken a drink from a wild fountain
    Early in the year;
There is nowhere to go from the top of a mountain
    But down, my dear;
And the springs that flow on the floor of the valley
    Will never seem fresh or clear
For thinking of the glitter of the mountain water
    In the feathery green of the year.

AT TINTAGIL

Iseult, Iseult, by the long waterways
    Watching the wintry moon, white as a flower,
I have remembered how once in Tintagil
    You heard the tread of Time hour after hour.

By casements hung with night, while all your women slept
    You turned toward Brittany, awake, alone,
In the high chamber hushed, save where the candle dripped
    With the slow patient sound of blood on stone.

The ache of empty arms was an old tale to you,
    And all the tragic tunes that love can play,
Yet with no woman born would you have changed your lot,
    Though there were greater queens who had been gay.

"THERE WILL BE STARS"

There will be stars over the place forever;
    Though the house we loved and the street we loved are lost,
Every time the earth circles her orbit
    On the night the autumn equinox is crossed,
Two stars we knew, poised on the peak of midnight
    Will reach their zenith; stillness will be deep;
There will be stars over the place forever,
    There will be stars forever, while we sleep.

II

PICTURES OF AUTUMN

AUTUMN
(Parc Monceau)

I shall remember only these leaves falling
    Small and incessant in the still air,
Yellow leaves on the dark green water resting
    And the marble Venus there—
Is she pointing to her breasts or trying to hide them?
    There is no god to care.

The colonnade curves close to the leaf-strewn water
    And its reflection seems
Lost in the mass of leaves and unavailing
    As a dream lost among dreams;
The colonnade curves close to the leaf-strewn water
    A dream lost among dreams.

SEPTEMBER DAY
(Pont de Neuilly)

The Seine flows out of the mist
    And into the mist again;
The trees lean over the water,
    The small leaves fall like rain.

The leaves fall patiently,
    Nothing remembers or grieves;
The river takes to the sea
    The yellow drift of the leaves.

Milky and cold is the air,
    The leaves float with the stream,
The river comes out of a sleep
    And goes away in a dream.

FONTAINEBLEAU

Interminable palaces front on the green parterres,
 And ghosts of ladies lovely and immoral
Glide down the gilded stairs,
 The high cold corridors are clicking with the heel taps
That long ago were theirs.

But in the sunshine, in the vague autumn sunshine,
 The geometric gardens are desolately gay;
The crimson and scarlet and rose-red dahlias
 Are painted like the ladies who used to pass this way
With a ringletted monarch, a Henry or a Louis
 On a lost October day.

The aisles of the garden lead into the forest,
 The aisles lead into autumn, a damp wind grieves,
Ghostly kings are hunting, the boar breaks cover,
 But the sounds of horse and horn are hushed in falling
  leaves,
 Four centuries of autumns, four centuries of leaves.

LATE OCTOBER
(Bois de Boulogne)

Listen, the damp leaves on the walks are blowing
 With a ghost of sound;
Is it a fog or is it a rain dripping
 From the low trees to the ground?

If I had gone before, I could have remembered
 Lilacs and green after-noons of May;
I chose to wait, I chose to hear from autumn
 Whatever she has to say.

III

SAND DRIFT

"BEAUTIFUL, PROUD SEA"

Careless forever, beautiful proud sea,
  You laugh in happy thunder all alone,
You fold upon yourself, you dance your dance
  Impartially on drift-weed, sand or stone.

You make us believe that we can outlive death,
  You make us for an instant, for your sake,
Burn, like stretched silver of a wave,
  Not breaking, but about to break.

LAND'S END

The shores of the world are ours, the solitary
  Beaches that bear no fruit, nor any flowers,
Only the harsh sea-grass that the wind harries
  Hours on unbroken hours.

No one will envy us these empty reaches
  At the world's end, and none will care that we
Leave our lost footprints where the sand forever
  Takes the unchanging passion of the sea.

SAND DRIFT

I thought I should not walk these dunes again,
  Nor feel the sting of this wind-bitten sand,
Where the coarse grasses always blow one way,
  Bent, as my thoughts are, by an unseen hand.

· · 231 · ·

I have returned; where the last wave rushed up
   The wet sand is a mirror for the sky
A bright blue instant, and along its sheen
   The nimble sandpipers run twinkling by.

Nothing has changed; with the same hollow thunder
   The waves die in their everlasting snow—
Only the place we sat is drifted over,
   Lost in the blowing sand, long, long ago.

BLUE STARGRASS

If we took the old path
   In the old field
The same gate would stand there
   That will never yield.

Where the sun warmed us
   With a cloak made of gold,
The rain would be falling
   And the wind would be cold;

And we would stop to search
   In the wind and the rain,
But we would not find the stargrass
   By the path again.

LOW TIDE

The birds are gathering over the dunes,
   Swerving and wheeling in shifting flight,
A thousand wings sweep darkly by
   Over the dunes and out of sight.

Why did you bring me down to the sea
    With the gathering birds and the fish-hawk flying,
The tide is low and the wind is hard,
    Nothing is left but the old year dying.

I wish I were one of the gathering birds,
    Two sharp black wings would be good for me—
When nothing is left but the old year dying,
    Why did you bring me down to the sea?

IV

PORTRAITS

EFFIGY OF A NUN
(Sixteenth Century)

Infinite gentleness, infinite irony
    Are in this face with fast-sealed eyes,
And round this mouth that learned in loneliness
    How useless their wisdom is to the wise.

In her nun's habit carved, patiently, lovingly,
    By one who knew the ways of womankind,
This woman's face still keeps, in its cold wistful calm,
    All of the subtle pride of her mind.

These long patrician hands, clasping the crucifix,
    Show she had weighed the world, her will was set;
These pale curved lips of hers, holding their hidden smile,
    Once having made their choice, knew no regret.

She was of those who hoard their own thoughts carefully,
    Feeling them far too dear to give away,
Content to look at life with the high, insolent
    Air of an audience watching a play.

If she was curious, if she was passionate
    She must have told herself that love was great,
But that the lacking it might be as great a thing
    If she held fast to it, challenging fate.

She who so loved herself and her own warring thoughts,
    Watching their humorous, tragic rebound,
In her thick habit's fold, sleeping, sleeping,
    Is she amused at dreams she has found?

Infinite tenderness, infinite irony
    Are hidden forever in her closed eyes,
Who must have learned too well in her long loneliness
    How empty wisdom is, even to the wise.

Those who love the most,
Do not talk of their love,
Francesca, Guinevere,
Deirdre, Iseult, Heloise,
In the fragrant gardens of heaven
Are silent, or speak if at all
Of fragile, inconsequent things.

And a woman I used to know
Who loved one man from her youth,
Against the strength of the fates
Fighting in somber pride,
Never spoke of this thing,
But hearing his name by chance,
A light would pass over her face.

EPITAPH

Serene descent, as a red leaf's descending
  When there is neither wind nor noise of rain,
But only autumn air and the unending
  Drawing of all things to the earth again:

So be it; let the snow sift deep and cover
  All that was drunken once with light and air;
The earth will not regret her tireless lover,
  Nor he awake to know she does not care.

APPRAISAL

Never think she loves him wholly,
Never believe her love is blind,
All his faults are locked securely
In a closet of her mind;
All his indecisions folded
Like old flags that time has faded,
Limp and streaked with rain,
And his cautiousness like garments
Frayed and thin, with many a stain—
Let them be, oh let them be,
There is treasure to outweigh them,
His proud will that sharply stirred,
Climbs as surely as the tide,
Senses strained too taut to sleep,
Gentleness to beast and bird,
Humor flickering hushed and wide
As the moon on moving water,
And a tenderness too deep
To be gathered in a word.

THE WISE WOMAN

She must be rich who can forego
    An hour so jewelled with delight,
She must have treasuries of joy
    That she can draw on day and night,
She must be very sure of heaven—
    Or is it only that she feels
How much more safe it is to lack
    A thing that time so often steals.

· · 239 · ·

"SHE WHO COULD BIND YOU"

She who could bind you
   Could bind fire to a wall;
She who could hold you
   Could hold a waterfall;
She who could keep you
   Could keep the wind from blowing
On a warm spring night
   With a low moon glowing.

V

MIDSUMMER NIGHTS

TWILIGHT

(Nahant)

There was an evening when the sky was clear,
  Ineffably translucent in its blue;
  The tide was falling and the sea withdrew
In hushed and happy music from the sheer
Shadowy granite of the cliffs; and fear
  Of what life may be, and what death can do,
  Fell from us like steel armor, and we knew
The wisdom of the Law that holds us here.
It was as though we saw the Secret Will,
  It was as though we floated and were free;
    In the south-west a planet shone serenely,
    And the high moon, most reticent and queenly,
Seeing the earth had darkened and grown still,
  Misted with light the meadows of the sea.

FULL MOON

(Santa Barbara)

I listened, there was not a sound to hear
  In the great rain of moonlight pouring down,
The eucalyptus trees were carved in silver,
  And a light mist of silver lulled the town.

I saw far off the grey Pacific bearing
  A broad white disk of flame,
And on the garden-walk a snail beside me
  Tracing in crystal the slow way he came.

· · 243 · ·

THE FOUNTAIN

Fountain, fountain, what do you say
    Singing at night alone?
"It is enough to rise and fall
    Here in my basin of stone."

But are you content as you seem to be
So near the freedom and rush of the sea?
    "I have listened all night to its laboring sound,
    It heaves and sags, as the moon runs round;
Ocean and fountain, shadow and tree,
Nothing escapes, nothing is free."

CLEAR EVENING

The crescent moon is large enough to linger
    A little while after the twilight goes,
This moist midsummer night the garden perfumes
    Are earth and apple, dewy pine and rose.

Over my head four new-cut stars are glinting
    And the inevitable night draws on;
I am alone, the old terror takes me,
    Evenings will come like this when I am gone;

Evenings on evenings, years on years forever—
    Be taut, my spirit, close upon and keep
The scent, the brooding chill, the gliding fire-fly,
    A poem learned before I fall asleep.

"NOT BY THE SEA"

Not by the sea, but somewhere in the hills,
Not by the sea, but in the uplands surely
There must be rest where a dim pool demurely
Watches all night the stern slow-moving skies;

Not by the sea, that never was appeased,
Not by the sea, whose immemorial longing
Shames the tired earth where even longing dies,
Not by the sea that bore Iseult and Helen,
But in a dark green hollow of the hills
There must be sleep, even for sleepless eyes.

MIDSUMMER NIGHT

Midsummer night without a moon, but the stars
    In a serene bright multitude were there,
Even the shyest ones, even the faint motes shining
    Low in the north, under the Little Bear.

When I have said, "This tragic farce I play in
    Has neither dignity, delight nor end,"
The holy night draws all its stars around me,
    I am ashamed, I have betrayed my Friend.

VI

THE CRYSTAL GAZER

THE CRYSTAL GAZER

I shall gather myself into myself again,
　I shall take my scattered selves and make them one,
Fusing them into a polished crystal ball
　Where I can see the moon and the flashing sun.

I shall sit like a sibyl, hour after hour intent,
　Watching the future come and the present go,
And the little shifting pictures of people rushing
　In restless self-importance to and fro.

THE SOLITARY

My heart has grown rich with the passing of years,
　I have less need now than when I was young
To share myself with every comer
　Or shape my thoughts into words with my tongue.

It is one to me that they come or go
　If I have myself and the drive of my will,
And strength to climb on a summer night
　And watch the stars swarm over the hill.

Let them think I love them more than I do,
　Let them think I care, though I go alone;
If it lifts their pride, what is it to me
　Who am self-complete as a flower or a stone.

DAY S ENDING

(Tucson)

Aloof as aged kings,
Wearing like them the purple,
The mountains ring the mesa
Crowned with a dusky light;
Many a time I watched
That coming-on of darkness
Till stars burned through the heavens
Intolerably bright.

It was not long I lived there
But I became a woman
Under those vehement stars,
For it was there I heard
For the first time my spirit
Forging an iron rule for me,
As though with slow cold hammers
Beating out word by word:

"Only yourself can heal you,
Only yourself can lead you,
The road is heavy going
And ends where no man knows;
Take love when love is given,
But never think to find it
A sure escape from sorrow
Or a complete repose."

A REPLY

Four people knew the very me,
Four is enough, so let it be;
For the rest I make no chart,
There are no highroads to my heart;
The gates are locked, they will not stir
For any ardent traveller.
I have not been misunderstood,
And on the whole, I think life good—
So waste no sympathy on me
Or any well-meant gallantry;
I have enough to do to muse
On memories I would not lose.

LEISURE

If I should make no poems any more
    There would be rest at least, so let it be;
Time to read books in other tongues and listen
    To the long mellow thunder of the sea.

The year will turn for me, I shall delight in
    All animals, and some of my own kind,
Sharing with no one but myself the frosty
    And half ironic musings of my mind.

"I SHALL LIVE TO BE OLD"

I shall live to be old, who feared I should die young,
    I shall live to be old.
I shall cling to life as the leaves to the creaking oak
    In the rustle of falling snow and the cold.

The other trees let loose their leaves on the air
    In their russet and red,
I have lived long enough to wonder which is the best,
    And to envy sometimes the way of the early dead.

WISDOM

It was a night of early spring,
    The winter-sleep was scarcely broken;
Around us shadows and the wind
    Listened for what was never spoken.

Though half a score of years are gone,
    Spring comes as sharply now as then—
But if we had it all to do
    It would be done the same again.

It was a spring that never came,
    But we have lived enough to know
What we have never had, remains;
    It is the things we have that go.

THE OLD ENEMY

Rebellion against death, the old rebellion
    Is over; I have nothing left to fight;
Battles have always had their meed of music
    But peace is quiet as a windless night.

Therefore I make no songs—I have grown certain
    Save when he comes too late, death is a friend,
A shepherd leading home his flock serenely
    Under the planet at the evening's end.

VII

BERKSHIRE NOTES

WINTER SUN
(Lenox)

There was a bush with scarlet berries
    And there were hemlocks heaped with snow;
With a sound like surf on long sea-beaches
    They took the wind and let it go.

The hills were shining in their samite,
    Fold after fold they flowed away—
"Let come what may," your eyes were saying,
    "At least we two have had to-day."

A DECEMBER DAY

Dawn turned on her purple pillow
    And late, late came the winter day,
Snow was curved to the boughs of the willow,
    The sunless world was white and gray.

At noon we heard a blue-jay scolding,
    At five the last thin light was lost
From snow-banked windows faintly holding
    The feathery filigree of frost.

FEBRUARY TWILIGHT

I stood beside a hill
    Smooth with new-laid snow,
A single star looked out
    From the cold evening glow.

There was no other creature
    That saw what I could see—
I stood and watched the evening star
    As long as it watched me.

Nothing is new, I have seen the spring too often;
There have been other plum-trees white as this one
Like a silvery cloud tethered beside the road,
I have been waked from sleep too many times
By birds at dawn boasting their love is beautiful.
The grass-blades gleam in the wind, nothing is changed.
Nothing is lost, it is all as it used to be,
Unopened lilacs are still as deep a purple,
The boughs of the elm are dancing still in a veil of tiny leaves,
Nothing is lost but a few years from my life.

WIND ELEGY
(W. E. W.)

Only the wind knows he is gone,
   Only the wind grieves,
The sun shines, the fields are sown,
   Sparrows mate in the eaves;

But I heard the wind in the pines he planted
   And the hemlocks overhead,
"His acres wake, for the year turns,
   But he is asleep," it said.

IN THE WOOD

I heard the water-fall rejoice
   Singing like a choir,
I saw the sun flash out of it
   Azure and amber fire.

The earth was like an open flower
    Enamelled and arrayed,
The path I took to find its heart
    Fluttered with sun and shade.

And while earth lured me, gently, gently,
    Happy and all alone,
Suddenly a heavy snake
    Reared black upon a stone.

AUTUMN DUSK

I saw above a sea of hills
    A solitary planet shine,
And there was no one near or far
    To keep the world from being mine.

VIII

ARCTURUS IN AUTUMN

ARCTURUS IN AUTUMN

When, in the gold October dusk, I saw you near to setting,
    Arcturus, bringer of spring,
Lord of the summer nights, leaving us now in autumn,
    Having no pity on our withering;

Oh then I knew at last that my own autumn was upon me,
    I felt it in my blood,
Restless as dwindling streams that still remember
    The music of their flood.

There in the thickening dark a wind-bent tree above me
    Loosed its last leaves in flight—
I saw you sink and vanish, pitiless Arcturus,
    You will not stay to share our lengthening night.

"I COULD SNATCH A DAY"

I could snatch a day out of the late autumn
    And set it trembling like forgotten springs,
There would be sharp blue skies with new leaves shining
    And flying shadows cast by flying wings.

I could take the heavy wheel of the world and break it,
    But we sit brooding while the ashes fall,
Cowering over an old fire that dwindles,
    Waiting for nothing at all.

AN END

I have no heart for any other joy,
    The drenched September day turns to depart,
And I have said good-bye to what I love;
    With my own will I vanquished my own heart.

On the long wind I hear the winter coming,
    The window panes are cold and blind with rain;
With my own will I turned the summer from me
    And summer will not come to me again.

FOREKNOWN

They brought me with a secret glee
    The news I knew before they spoke,
        And though they hoped to see me riven,
        They found me light as dry leaves driven
    Before the storm that splits an oak.

For I had learned from many an autumn
    The way a leaf can drift and go,
        Lightly, lightly, almost gay
        Taking the unreturning way
    To mix with winter and the snow.

WINTER

I shall have winter now and lessening days,
Lit by a smoky sun with slanting rays,
And after falling leaves, the first determined frost.
The colors of the world will all be lost.
So be it; the faint buzzing of the snow
Will fill the empty boughs,
And after sleet storms I shall wake to see
A glittering glassy plume of every tree.
Nothing shall tempt me from my fire-lit house,
And I shall find at night a friendly ember
And make my life of what I can remember.

WINTER NIGHT SONG

Will you come as of old with singing,
    And shall I hear as of old?
Shall I rush to open the window
    In spite of the arrowy cold?

    Ah no, my dear, ah no,
        I shall sit by the fire reading,
    Though you sing half the night in the snow
        I shall not be heeding.

Though your voice remembers the forest,
    The warm green light and the birds,
Though you gather the sea in your singing
    And pour its sound into words,

    Even so, my dear, even so,
        I shall not heed you at all;
    Though your shoulders are white with snow,
        Though you strain your voice to a call,
    I shall drowse and the fire will drowse,
        The draught will be cold on the floor,
    The clock running down,
        Snow banking the door.

NEVER AGAIN

Never again the music blown as brightly
    Off of my heart as foam blown off a wave;
Never again the melody that lightly
    Caressed my grief and healed the wounds it gave.

Never again—I hear my dark thoughts clashing
  Sullen and blind as waves that beat a wall—
Age that is coming, summer that is going,
  All I have lost or never found at all.

THE TUNE

I know a certain tune that my life plays;
  Over and over I have heard it start
With all the wavering loveliness of viols
  And gain in swiftness like a runner's heart.

It climbs and climbs; I watch it sway in climbing
  High over time, high even over doubt,
It has all heaven to itself—it pauses
  And faltering blindly down the air, goes out.

IX

THE FLIGHT

THE BELOVED

It is enough of honor for one lifetime
   To have known you better than the rest have known,
The shadows and the colors of your voice,
   Your will, immutable and still as stone.

The shy heart, so lonely and so gay,
   The sad laughter and the pride of pride,
The tenderness, the depth of tenderness
   Rich as the earth, and wide as heaven is wide.

"WHEN I AM NOT WITH YOU"

When I am not with you
I am alone,
For there is no one else
And there is nothing
That comforts me but you.
When you are gone
Suddenly I am sick,
Blackness is round me,
There is nothing left.
I have tried many things,
Music and cities,
Stars in their constellations
And the sea,
But there is nothing
That comforts me but you;
And my poor pride bows down
Like grass in a rain-storm

Drenched with my longing.
The night is unbearable,
Oh let me go to you
For there is no one,
There is nothing
To comfort me but you.

ON A MARCH DAY

Here in the teeth of this triumphant wind
   That shakes the naked shadows on the ground,
Making a key-board of the earth to strike
   From clattering tree and hedge a separate sound,

Bear witness for me that I loved my life,
   All things that hurt me and all things that healed,
And that I swore to it this day in March,
   Here at the edge of this new-broken field.

You only knew me, tell them I was glad
   For every hour since my hour of birth,
And that I ceased to fear, as once I feared,
   The last complete reunion with the earth.

"LET IT BE YOU"

Let it be you who lean above me
   On my last day,
Let it be you who shut my eyelids
   Forever and aye.

Say a "Good-night" as you have said it
    All of these years,
With the old look, with the old whisper
    And without tears.

You will know then all that in silence
    You always knew,
Though I have loved, I loved no other
    As I love you.

THE FLIGHT

We are two eagles
Flying together
Under the heavens,
Over the mountains,
Stretched on the wind.
Sunlight heartens us,
Blind snow baffles us,
Clouds wheel after us
Ravelled and thinned.

We are like eagles,
But when Death harries us,
Human and humbled
When one of us goes,
Let the other follow,
Let the flight be ended,
Let the fire blacken,
Let the book close.

Stars To-night

VERSES FOR BOYS AND GIRLS

(1930)

NIGHT

Stars over snow
   And in the west a planet
Swinging below a star—
   Look for a lovely thing and you will find it,
It is not far—
   It never will be far.

LATE OCTOBER

I found ten kinds of wild flowers growing
On a steely day that looked like snowing:
Queen Anne's lace, and blue heal-all,
A buttercup, straggling, grown too tall,
A rusty aster, a chicory flower—
Ten I found in half an hour.
The air was blurred with dry leaves flying,
Gold and scarlet, gaily dying.
A squirrel ran off with a nut in his mouth,
And always, always, flying south,
Twittering, the birds went by
Flickering sharp against the sky,
Some in great bows, some in wedges,
Some in bands with wavering edges;
Flocks and flocks were flying over
With the north wind for their drover.
"Flowers," I said, "you'd better go,
Surely it's coming on for snow,"—
They did not heed me, nor heed the birds,
Twittering thin, far-fallen words—
The others thought of to-morrow, but they
Only remembered yesterday.

THE FALLING STAR

I saw a star slide down the sky,
Blinding the north as it went by,
Too burning and too quick to hold,
Too lovely to be bought or sold,
Good only to make wishes on
And then forever to be gone.

THE SPICEBUSH IN MARCH

Spicebush, yellow spicebush, tell me
    Where you found so much clear gold?
Every branch and every twig
    Has as much as it can hold,
Flaunting before tattered winter
    Your new dress the wind whips round—
Color, color! You were first,
    You dredged and drew it from the ground!

CALM MORNING AT SEA

Midocean like a pale blue morning-glory
    Opened wide, wide;
The ship cut softly through the silken surface;
    We watched white sea-birds ride
Unrocking on the holy virgin water
    Fleckless on every side.

TO ARCTURUS RETURNING

Arcturus, with the spring returning,
    I love you best; I cannot tell
Why, save that your recurrent burning
    Is spring's most punctual miracle.

You bring with you all longed-for things,
    Birds with their song, leaves with their stir,
And you, beyond all other stars,
    Have been man's comforter.

A JUNE DAY

I heard a red-winged black-bird singing
    Down where the river sleeps in the reeds;
That was morning, and at noontime
    A humming-bird flashed on the jewel-weeds;
Clouds blew up, and in the evening
    A yellow sunset struck through the rain,
Then blue night, and the day was ended
    That never will come again.

RHYME OF NOVEMBER STARS

The noiseless marching of the stars
Sweeps above me all night long;
Up the skies, over the skies,
Passes the uncounted throng,
Without haste, without rest,
From the east to the west:

Vega, Deneb, white Altair
Shine like crystals in the air,
And the lonely Fomalhaut
In the dark south, paces low.
Now the timid Pleiades
Leave the shelter of the trees,
While toward the north, mounting high,
Gold Capella, like a queen,
Watches over her demesne
Stretching toward the kingly one,
Dusky, dark Aldebaran.
Betelguese and Rigel burn
In their wide wheel, slow to turn,
And in the sharp November frost
Bright Sirius, with his blue light
Completes the loveliness of night.

I STOOD UPON A STAR

I stretched my mind until I stood
   Out in space, upon a star;
I looked, and saw the flying earth
   Where seven planets are.

Delicately interweaving
   Like fireflies on a moist June night,
The planetoids among the planets
   Played for their own delight.

I watched earth putting off her winter
   And slipping into green;
I saw the dark side of the moon
   No man has ever seen.

Like shining wheels in an opened watch
   They all revolved with soundless motion;
Earth sparkled like a rain-wet flower,
   Bearing her petals, plain and ocean.

WINTER NOON

Snow-dust driven over the snow
   In glittering light,
Low hills, far as the eye can go,
   White on white;
Blue as a blue jay, shadows run
   Due north from every tree—
Chipmunk, do you like the sun,
   The blowing snow and me?

Strange Victory
(1933)

I

MOON'S ENDING

Moon, worn thin to the width of a quill,
    In the dawn clouds flying,
How good to go, light into light, and still
    Giving light, dying.

WISDOM

Oh to relinquish, with no more of sound
Than the bent bough's when the bright apples fall;
Oh to let go, without a cry or call
That can be heard by any above ground;
Let the dead know, but not the living see—
The dead who loved me will not suffer, knowing
It is all one, the coming or the going,
If I have kept the last, essential me.
If that is safe, then I am safe indeed,
It is my citadel, my church, my home,
My mother and my child, my constant friend;
It is my music, making for my need
A pæan like the cymbals of the foam,
Or silence, level, spacious, without end.

AUTUMN ON THE BEACHES

Not more blue at the dawn of the world,
    Not more virgin or more gay,
Never in all the million years
    Was the sea happier than to-day.

The sand was not more trackless then,
   Morning more stainless or more cold—
Only the forest and the fields
   Know that the year is old.

ADVICE TO A GIRL

No one worth possessing
Can be quite possessed;
Lay that on your heart,
My young angry dear;
This truth, this hard and precious stone,
Lay it on your hot cheek,
Let it hide your tear.
Hold it like a crystal
When you are alone
And gaze in the depths of the icy stone.
Long, look long and you will be blessed:
No one worth possessing
Can be quite possessed.

AGE

Brooks sing in the spring
   And in summer cease;
I who sang in my youth
   Now hold my peace;
Youth is a noisy stream
   Chattering over the ground,
But the sad wisdom of age
   Wells up without sound.

EVEN TO-DAY

What if the bridge men built goes down,
What if the torrent sweeps the town,
The hills are safe, the hills remain,
And hills are happy in the rain;
If I can climb the hills and find
A small square cottage to my mind,
A lonely but a cleanly house
With shelves too bare to tempt a mouse,
Whatever years remain to me
I shall live out in dignity.

TRUCE

Take heart, for now the battle is half over,
    We have not shamed our sires;
Pride, the lone pennon, ravelled by the storm-wind
    Stands in the sunset fires.

It may be, with the coming-on of evening
    We shall be granted unassailed repose,
And what is left of dusk will be less darkness
    Than luminous air, on which the crescent glows.

II

STRANGE VICTORY

To this, to this, after my hope was lost,
   To this strange victory;
To find you with the living, not the dead,
   To find you glad of me;
To find you wounded even less than I,
   Moving as I across the stricken plain;
After the battle to have found your voice
   Lifted above the slain.

SECRET TREASURE

Fear not that my music seems
Like water locked in winter streams;
You are the sun that many a time
Thawed those rivers into rhyme,
But let them for a while remain
A hidden music in my brain.

Unmeaning phrase and wordless measure,
That unencumbered loveliness
Which is a poet's secret treasure
Sings in me now, and sings no less
That even for your lenient eyes
It will not live in written guise.

LAST PRELUDE

If this shall be the last time
The melody flies upward
With its rush of sparks in flight,
Let me go up with it in fire and laughter,
Or let me drown if need be
Lost in the swirl of light.

The violins are tuning, whimpering, catching thunder
From the suppressed dark agony of viols—
Once more let heaven clutch me, plunge me under
Miles on uncounted miles.

IN A DARKENING GARDEN

Gather together, against the coming of night,
    All that we played with here,
Toys and fruits, the quill from the sea-bird's flight,
    The small flute, hollow and clear;
The apple that was not eaten, the grapes untasted—
    Let them be put away.
They served for us, I would not have them wasted,
    They lasted out our day.

TO M.

Till the last sleep, from the blind waking at birth,
    Bearing the weight of the years between the two,
I shall find no better thing upon the earth
    Than the wilful, noble, faulty thing which is you.

You have not failed me; but if you too should fail me,
    Being human, bound on your own inviolate quest,
No matter now what the years do to assail me
    I shall go, in some sort, a victor, down to my rest.

ASHES

Laid in a quiet corner of the world,
There will be left no more of me some night
Than the lone bat could carry in his flight
Over the meadows when the moon is furled;
I shall be then so little, and so lost,
Only the many-fingered rain will find me,
And I have taken thought to leave behind me
Nothing to feel the long on-coming frost.

Now without sorrow and without elation
I can lay down my body, nor deplore
How little, with her insufficient ration,
Life has to feed us—but these hands, must they
Go in the same blank, ignominious way,
And fold upon themselves, at last, no more?

IN MEMORY OF VACHEL LINDSAY

"Deep in the ages," you said, "deep in the ages,"
  And, "To live in mankind is far more than to live in a
    name."
You are deep in the ages, now, deep in the ages,
  You whom the world could not break, nor the years tame.

Fly out, fly on, eagle that is not forgotten,
  Fly straight to the innermost light, you who loved sun in
    your eyes,
Free of the fret, free of the weight of living,
  Bravest among the brave, gayest among the wise.

GRACE BEFORE SLEEP

How can our minds and bodies be
Grateful enough that we have spent
Here in this generous room, we three,
This evening of content?
Each one of us has walked through storm
And fled the wolves along the road;
But here the hearth is wide and warm,
And for this shelter and this light
Accept, O Lord, our thanks to-night.

III

"ALL THAT WAS MORTAL"

All that was mortal shall be burned away,
    All that was mind shall have been put to sleep.
Only the spirit shall awake to say
    What the deep says to the deep;
But for an instant, for it too is fleeting—
    As on a field with new snow everywhere,
Footprints of birds record a brief alighting
    In flight begun and ended in the air.

TO THE SEA

Bitter and beautiful, sing no more;
Scarf of spindrift strewn on the shore,
Burn no more in the noon-day light,
Let there be night for me, let there be night.

On the restless beaches I used to range
The two that I loved have walked with me—
I saw them change and my own heart change—
I cannot face the unchanging sea.

RETURN TO A COUNTRY HOUSE

Nothing but darkness enters in this room,
Nothing but darkness and the winter night,
Yet on this bed once years ago a light
Silvered the sheets with an unearthly bloom;
It was the planet Venus in the west
Casting a square of brightness on this bed,
And in that light your dark and lovely head
Lay for a while and seemed to be at rest.

But that the light is gone, and that no more
Even if it were here, would you be here,—
That is one line in a long tragic play
That has been acted many times before,
And acted best when not a single tear
Falls,—when the mind and not the heart holds sway.

"SINCE DEATH BRUSHED PAST ME"

Since Death brushed past me once more to-day,
Let me say quickly what I must say:
Take without shame the love I give you,
Take it before I am hurried away.

You are intrepid, noble, kind,
My heart goes to you with my mind,
The plummet of your thought is long
Sunk in deep water, cold with song.
You are all I asked, my dear—
My words are said, my way is clear.

TO A CHILD WATCHING THE GULLS
(Queenstown Harbor)

The painted light was on their underwings,
    And on their firm curved breasts the painted light,
Sailing they swerved in the red air of sunset
    With petulant cries unworthy of their flight;
But on their underwings that fleeting splendor,
    Those chilly breasts an instant burning red—
You who are young, O you who will outlive me,
    Remember them for the indifferent dead.

· · 296 · ·

LINES

These are the ultimate highlands,
Like chord on chord of music
Climbing to rest
On the highest peak and the bluest
Large on the luminous heavens
Deep in the west.

"THERE WILL BE REST"

There will be rest, and sure stars shining
   Over the roof-tops crowned with snow,
A reign of rest, serene forgetting,
   The music of stillness holy and low.

I will make this world of my devising
   Out of a dream in my lonely mind,
I shall find the crystal of peace,—above me
   Stars I shall find.

INDEX TO FIRST LINES

· · 303 · ·